Holy Places, Sacred Sites

To all the friends who,
when I most needed them,
were by my side

Eduardo Rubio

PHOTOGRAPHS, FOREWORD AND CAPTIONS **Eduardo Rubio Méndez**

INTRODUCTION, TEXT AND EPILOGUE **Juan Masiá Clavel**

Holy Places, Sacred Sites

*A Journey to the World's
Most Spiritual Locations*

WITH OVER 300 COLOUR ILLUSTRATIONS

 Thames & Hudson

First published in the United Kingdom in 2008 by Thames & Hudson Ltd, 181A High Holborn, London WC1V 7QX

www.thamesandhudson.com

British Library Cataloguing-in-Publication Data
A catalogue record for this book is available from the British Library

ISBN: 978-0-500-51449-8

Printed and bound in Spain

CONTENTS

Then Vidagdha Sâkalya asked him:

'How many gods are there, O Yâgñavalkya?'

He replied with this very Nivid:

'As many as are mentioned in the Nivid of the hymn of praise addressed to the Visvedevas, viz. three and three hundred, three and three thousand.'

'Yes,' he said, and asked again:

'How many gods are there really, O Yâgñavalkya?'

'Thirty-three,' he said.

'Yes,' he said, and asked again:

'How many gods are there really, O Yâgñavalkya?'

'Six,' he said.

'Yes,' he said, and asked again:

'How many gods are there really, O Yâgñavalkya?'

'Three,' he said.

'Yes,' he said, and asked again:

'How many gods are there really, O Yâgñavalkya?'

'Two,' he said.

'Yes,' he said, and asked again:

'How many gods are there really, O Yâgñavalkya?'

'One and a half,' he said.

'Yes,' he said, and asked again:

'How many gods are there really, O Yâgñavalkya?'

'One,' he said.

BRIHADARANYAKA UPANISHAD III, 9, I

FOREWORD

My mother, just like all mothers, will go to heaven.

She believes in paradise, even though she doesn't say what it's like, or where it is.

My mother is convinced that when she gets to heaven, she will meet her deceased husband and her daughters. My father and my sisters.

Believing in heaven, and all that that involves, helps her to live, and it will help her to die.

I think it is wonderful that my mother, just like almost every mother, believes in heaven. I don't know whether I believe in it, even though I'd like it to exist. Just like many sons and daughters would.

I don't even know whether that marvellous heaven – where I would meet up with my dead father, sisters and friends – even exists. There are as many things that make me believe in it as there are that tell me that it is impossible.

I would like to believe, but I don't know how to manage it.

But one thing's certain: my mother will definitely go to heaven, and she will meet up with all her loved ones. I'm sure of it. I know it.

'IF YOU WANT TO MAKE GOD LAUGH, TELL HIM YOUR PLANS'

With this Sufi thought in my head, one fine day in 2004, I went into action. My plan was an ambitious, complex one, and no doubt more than one god had a good laugh about it: I was going to search for God and the gods, as well as the people who believe in them, and live with them and off them.

I had to immerse myself in the world of religions, their believers and devotees. I had to travel to the sacred places of the Earth and to explore a whole host of legends in which gods (with a variety of names and sur-names) competed to be the most powerful beings before those men and women who wanted or needed to believe.

It is said that there are over a thousand religions practised today.

As a travelling companion, I took my Nikon, while I packed my suitcase with all manner of books and papers, information and tales, places, names, dates and history.

I spent three exciting years wandering through the world of the hereafter, during which time I chalked up hundreds of hours of air travel, thousands of kilometres on the roads, more than 50,000 stories and the occasional photograph or two.

On my journey, I met some wonderful people – people who believed or needed to believe in something. Human beings, like me, who sought in their gods meaning, explanations, consolation...a miracle, even.

On that same journey I also met up with fanatics, visionaries whose egos were fed by people of good faith, people who were ignorant, weak and stupid. There is a place for everyone.

I lived among Catholics, Muslims, Buddhists and Jews. I had encounters with Parsees, Taoists, Jainists and many other believers who had their own God and their own truths, rites, hopes and fears.

At some point, all of them almost managed to persuade me.

But none of them succeeded in showing me a path that was truly new, different, or surprising.

DOES GOD EXIST?

I would like to have an answer to this question. But I haven't.

I don't know anyone who has returned from the hereafter in order to ask them to explain what it's all about.

Either you have faith, or you cannot get close to God.

Either you believe or you don't. It's all right to want to believe, but not to ask for explanations about the world of the afterlife. Did God create man? Is God one of our creations? Are there many gods, even a family of them? Do they get on well, or not? Do they imitate us, or do we imitate them? Are they good or evil? Should I believe? A lot or just a little? Should I believe everything or nothing?

My mother believes in God. Millions of human beings believe in God.

It must be out of necessity. Or out of fear.

During the course of my life, I have sometimes felt that He exists. I have also felt the opposite.

I gave Him thanks for keeping me safe from the bullets in Chechnya, and on the day my daughter was born.

I angrily demanded an explanation from Him each time one of my loved ones died – Isabel, Carmen, María Jesús, Antonio, Jacinto and Jaime.

I rebelled against Him when I saw children dying of hunger in Ethiopia. If You are good and generous, I thought, why do You allow this to happen?

I found it difficult to understand Him when I witnessed, horrified, real barbarity at first hand: in the name of a god, many people are killed in many parts of the world.

But a death is a death, in the name of whoever.

The cross and the half-moon should never be mixed with the sword.

If God exists...how can he allow all this to happen?

There is always the contradiction.

MARIA, TRY TO BE MORE OF A RESPECTER THAN A BELIEVER

Maria is ten years old. She's my daughter.

Whenever I can, I take her with me on my travels through the world.

I like to write a few words for her in each of my books.

Maria and I have talked about God and gods.

It is hard for me to know to what extent she understands the subject, or understands me. It is difficult to talk to a child about something that you can't comprehend yourself.

I don't know whether I want my daughter to grow up with the idea of a god who is magical, powerful and controls life and death. Instead, I try to help her to find a god, her god. After that she can continue down her own path.

I know that one day, she will feel something. Just as we all have.

She will have found her god, and she – and she alone – will give this god a name, an appearance and powers. No doubt, she will seek a way of communicating with her god.

I would like Maria to be more of a respecter than a believer. I should like it if her mind and soul were open to everything and everyone. Without any fanaticism, obsession or imposition. Without following any credos, masters or visionaries.

I would like Maria to be a good soul.

Just like the soul that most of us have within us.

With the help of a god or without it.

Maybe we are the gods?

EDUARDO RUBIO MÉNDEZ
Barcelona, March 2008

INTRODUCTION

How will readers react to these photographs? With curiosity, with surprise, or with a smile? Neither the photographer nor the publisher know for certain. The only thing that I can be sure of is the way that I react to them personally. After thinking hard, over and over again, about the images in this volume – sometimes calmly enjoying them, sometimes feeling uneasy about not being able to discern an answer to the questions they present – I believe the central experience can be summed up in one word: perplexity. In the name of a god, wonders are produced. In the name of a god, barbarous acts are committed. Why?

The question is a perennial one, but it is a fact that these photographs reflect the paradox of man's relationship with what we call the world of sacredness. We allow ourselves to become absorbed into it, escaping from ourselves as it leads us toward the ultimate secret of life, a form of nirvana. But if we try to manipulate it, we may be sucked into a vortex of death and ceaseless violence. And it all happens within the same space: 'How terrible is this place! This is none other but the house of God, and the gate of Heaven', as Jacob said [Genesis 28: 17]. But he could also have said: 'How dangerous is this place! This is none other but the gate to the abyss'.

The paradoxes of holiness, in the name of which both good and evil are done, are reflected in the contrasting variety of faces, images, landscapes, architectures – in short, all the supposedly sacred places – that appear in these photographs.

The genius of this photographer lies in his ability to capture the paradoxical essence of these spaces. The settings portrayed here are neither abstract nor geometric. Rather, they are spaces of nature and humanity, landscapes and rural areas imbued with an atmosphere that flows from within them; they refer to what we call (in the absence of any other term) 'sacredness'. These spaces are not merely places of worship or congregation, they are also epiphanic sites of spirituality that provoke, evoke and promise paths leading towards a meeting with the ultimate meaning of everything.

The ambiguity of sacredness

But holiness is ambiguous: simultaneously fascinating and terrible, it both seduces and terrifies us. Through this miscellany of images and symbols, and the faces of supplicants and grateful believers, this collection of photographs forces the viewer to confront the paradox of specific, historical manifestations of our relationship with holiness: exhortations of peace and declarations of war, slogans of concord and shouts of violence. In the name of holiness, the unforgivable is forgiven, and the incompatible is reconciled, but that same name is also used to unleash phobias, persecutions, fanaticisms and violent conflict.

This book makes the viewer acknowledge the dual reality of our conception of sacredness. While hands clasped together might suggest worship, they can also denote superstition. While the darkness of the forest invites us to submerge ourselves in the heart of a welcoming mystery, it also breeds nightmares about violated taboos and vengeful gods. While high peaks encourage us to build hermitages or altars facing Heaven, the view down into the precipice makes us giddy with vertigo. While the ocean might suggest infinity to us (as Leopardi says, 'It is sweet to become shipwrecked'), the strong northwesterly wind is threatening and makes us fear that Leviathan is about to appear. While crowds of pilgrims passing by impress us with their faith, it is frightening to think how easily and suddenly a fervent procession could become transformed into an anarchic horde of terrorists.

Paradoxes of holiness

Hence my perplexity. I see the dual face of holiness – sometimes peaceful, sometimes worrying – reflected in the ambivalent appearance of many images. Just as it is easy to feel overwhelmed by the plurality of expressions of spirituality, from the sublime to the crude, one can also be left disconcerted by the many paradoxes in the world of sacredness.

For example, there is the paradox of trying to make visible what is invisible. 'No one has ever seen God', says the Gospel according to John – except for Jesus, who lived, 'in the bosom of the Father, he hath declared him' [John 1: 18].

There is the paradox of the death of God, which becomes so necessary for us after the demise of the many false and inauthentic images of reality that have been instilled in us, or which we have invented.

There is the paradox of the drop of water on the tip of the Buddha's index finger. What would you do to prevent it from evaporating? How could you preserve it forever? What lengths would you go to in order not to lose it? The answer is very easy: just dip the finger into the sea.

There is the paradox of the ascents and descents that can be found along the inner path; they are not staircases, tunnels or passageways of initiation, but thresholds of transformation: John of the Cross in the deepest darkness on Mount Carmel; Teresa of Avila penetrating the castle of the soul, step-by-step. They transcend to the bottom, submerging themselves in the chasms of awareness, in the Buddhist schools of Yogacara.

And in all these inner journeys, there is the paradox of dark nights and the dawn of rebirth.

There is the paradox of the mystic who must humble himself before the poet, and the moralistic theologian who is in turn displaced by the mystic.

There is the paradox of the bread and the wine, which were already sacred – sustaining divine life – without us realizing it. Yet a creative word reveals their symbolism, and gives them a new meaning.

There is the paradox of religiosity, which is at once both far removed and yet very close to religion. How much latent spirituality there is even without the existence of denominations!

There is the paradox of Buddha and Jesus. They are not founders, they leave no written documents, they do answer key questions, they are treated as atheists...but they remain imperturbable, animated and led by an impulse that could be called *Dharma* (in the language of Buddhism) or *Pneuma* (in the language of Christianity) – that is, the Way, or the Spirit.

There is paradox of the unity of the Mystery, and the plurality of its manifestations. There is no need to syncretize religions, or to create a common Esperanto of their languages. There is only one sun, but there are many stained glass windows that filter the sunlight differently, according to the colours of their glass and the interior space that receives the light.

There is the paradox of the institutionalized administration of religions: the more moralizing they are, the less good they are; the clearer and more different they are, the less true they are; the more symmetrical they are, the less artistic; the tenser they are, the less they believe.

There is the paradox of meetings and disagreements between the different forms of religiosity and spirituality. Disagreements that take place right across the surface of the earth, whenever attempts are made to bring them together or to greet opposite numbers. Encounters in the centre of the globe when each radial line travels down toward a single point.

Marriage in widowhood?

Fifty-nine-year-old Tanaka is a Japanese widower whose children are already married, and who has taken early retirement. In Florence, he meets Lina, a 54-year-old Italian woman, also widowed, and whose children are also married. What they have in common is that they both like art and they like each other; they strike up a relationship and end up living together. It would not have been the same had they met up, as their first love, when he went to study in Italy at the age of 22. One cannot say that the relationship is worse or better – it is simply different, because they both have a lot of history – their respective life stories – behind them. This new relationship will mature (or not) depending on whether these stories converge from this point on. In the best of cases, perhaps they will be mutually transformed as they embark on a common project for the future.

This parable can help us to focus on the relationship between two religions that meet up after each has amassed several centuries of history. For example, the current ongoing encounter between Buddhism and Christianity. It would have been different had it taken place one-and-a-half or two millennia ago. Had it happened then, perhaps the symbolism of the Trinity would bear a greater similarity to the doctrine on the three bodies of the Buddha in Mayan Buddhism. But that is not what happened, and history is history. And so, now that this encounter has finally taken place, it bears an enormous burden in terms of both culture and tradition, from the Councils of Nicea and Chalcedony of the 4th and 5th centuries to the papal encyclicals of the 19th and 20th centuries. In the 21st century, the task will be to organize possible integrations of Christianity and Buddhism, perhaps with fewer words and more significant silences. But who would be capable, for example, of harmoniously linking the Buddhas seen in this book with the imagery of the Virgin of Fátima or the saccharine-sweet 19th-century Sacred Heart of Jesus? Or who could establish a bridge of communication between a Tibetan lama concentrating on the silence of his cell and the shouts and cries of an excited crowd dancing to the beat of a neoconservative preacher?

Neither tourism nor proselytism

Presenting this project merely as a kind of religious tourism – a kind of 'journey around the world of sacredness in 80 days' – would be a superficial approach. Admittedly, the international diversity of photographs, and the juxtaposition of faces, landscapes and different styles of architecture could invite such an interpretation (though for a journey like that there would be no need for saddlebags or knapsacks – travel agencies, with their powers of advertising, take care of all of that). But it would be naive to use these images to promote the preachings and beliefs of one religious denomination over another. Instead, they should be used as a platform for inter-religious encounters that go beyond religions and their social and historical forms, in an attempt to glimpse the future of spirituality.

A popular procession in the streets of La Paz, Bolivia

I use the word 'encounter' intentionally. An encounter means more than dialogue, and less than conversion. When I chat with my good friend Master Suzuki, the head of a Buddhist community in Tokyo's Nerima district, I do not try to convert him to Christianity, nor does he try to convert me to Buddhism. But both of us agree that after our conversations the Buddhist has the sensation of being simultaneously 'more and less Buddhist' than he was prior to the encounter, while the Christian also feels 'more and less Christian' – more Christian in the sense that I have rediscovered forgotten aspects of my Christianity; 'less Christian' because I have been forced to rid myself of many of the historical convictions and traditional excrescences of my western Christianity.

East and West

As Raimon Panikkar says, the West must discover its own interior East. The encounter between East and West should be one of mutual transformation which leads to an undoing and a remaking of their very identities. Religion can give people the strength to carry on living, but the vitality of religiousness can be discovered beyond the specific social and historical forms of the different religions. For example, at a meeting between Buddhists and Christians, both parties explore their own spirituality more deeply. As I have mentioned, the Christian is not converted to Buddhism, or vice versa; instead, both sides are transformed in their view of the mystery, while each one polishes and refines his own spirituality.

I attended the talks given by Professor Kojiro Tamaki – a Buddhist and an Emeritus Professor of Eastern Philosophy at Tokyo University – during the last years of his life. One of the central themes he always returned to was the four great spiritual figures of Buddha, Jesus, Confucius and Socrates (he must be excused for not including Muhammad, but the Prophet did not fall within his particular field). These four men, he used to say, were peaceful and peacemakers. All four did more through their deeds than their words; they were all viewed as suspicious by the established powers; they were considered to be atheists by the existing religions; they all invited people to step out of themselves, both inwards and outwards – inwards by means of meditation, and outwards through compassion and solidarity with others. All four figures exhorted people to stop and listen to the tiny voice inside their hearts that speaks the truth about us and about our lives. And all four encouraged the practice of reconciliation and liberation.

I feel sure that if Professor Tamaki saw these photographs, he would remind us once again of the importance of focusing on the common characteristics of these great masters of humanity, rather than becoming bogged down in the tiny details of each religion.

A pilgrimage through temples and landscapes

These photographs show many images of divine dwellings: temples, mosques, pagodas, cathedrals and basilicas. By way of contrast, there are also important sacred sites found in the heart of nature: rocks, ancient trees, desert landscapes and leafy forests. Throughout the course of history, man has fluctuated between a tendency to try to imprison sacredness in architectural constructions and to allow himself to be surrounded by holiness by identifying with nature.

Pilgrimages seem to combine both tendencies. The pilgrim journeys towards a certain place, towards an encounter with the divine in its special location. However, at the same time, the elusive presence of the divine can be detected during the journey itself: in the landscape, in the path, in the meetings pilgrims have on the way. Humans are inveterate travellers and wanderers – for this reason, they need to make pilgrimages and to narrate the journey. Pilgrims also need to build shelters

along the way, which represent sketchy foretastes of their objective. They may also be tempted to settle down in them. But the call of spirituality will bring exoduses, with people taking to the road and embarking on pilgrimages once again. This latent anthropological aspect has led us to link the group of photographs entitled 'Pilgrimages' with those entitled 'Dwellings of Holiness' and 'Landscapes of the Soul', respectively. All of them show the objectives and landscapes of spiritual pilgrimage. Of course, there are many different types of pilgrimage. But don't pilgrims from different religions sometimes meet up, halfway to their destination, even if they do not feel obliged to change their route as a consequence? And there lies the urgent, thorny issue – how to move from conflicts between religions to exchanges.

Embracing or conflicting?

Will all these very different photographs of the world of the sacred encourage religions to come together in a mutual embrace between varying beliefs, or in a fight between opponents?

The important issue to address is that of encouraging dialogue between different forms of spirituality. Perhaps it would be better to speak of 'encounters on the road' – meetings between different people, cultures and religions that still have some way to go before they finally come together, groups that do not have a monopoly on the path's objective, and who are mutually transformed as they carry on walking and seeking. At the beginning of the 21st century, humanity is embarked on a search for ways (as yet undiscovered) of living and expressing their spirituality and faith in unprecedented situations. Believers are discovering that they need to reformulate, renew and reinterpret their faith within the framework of new international, intercultural and inter-religious settings.

For example, with the *Nostra aetate* declaration of the Vatican II Council, the Catholic Church went from rejecting the values of other religions to acknowledging them, and since then the Vatican has not repeated the claim that 'there is no salvation outside the Church'. Later on a movement towards an inclusive approach began (in those days, believers of other religions tended to be viewed as 'anonymous Christians'). This inclusive approach had to be overcome in the face of the challenge of pluralism, though it still has not been fully digested today, and is being impeded by regressive actions from markedly neoconservative movements. At the same time, outbreaks of a new awareness can be perceived here and there, though they still have not fully taken shape.

Are we facing once more what the philosopher Karl Jaspers referred to as a kind of 'time-axis' in the history of humanity? Has the moment arrived when we have to discover new ways of expressing spirituality – a new, authentic interiorization, coupled with the rediscovery and reformulation of closeness, solidarity, compassionate and restorative justice and just peace? Or, rather, is it a question of refounding spirituality, just as many others – including Gautama, the Buddha, Lao Tse, Confucius, Mencius, Jeremiah, Hosea, Amos, Hillel the rabbi, Jesus of Nazareth, Socrates and Muhammad – did in their time?

Seen in this light, the enormous variety displayed in these photographs begins to make sense. As we turn the pages, we may feel encouraged to embark upon a pilgrimage of our own, in search of an objective that many have glimpsed, but nobody has controlled or monopolized. Miguel de Unamuno would have agreed with this view. He saw religiosity as an uninterrupted search, claiming in his essay 'My Relgion' that: 'My religion...is a search for the truth in life and life in the truth, while being aware that I do not have to find it during my lifetime; my religion is to fight tirelessly and ceaselessly with the mystery; my religion is to fight with God from the break of dawn to nightfall, as Jacob is said to have fought with Him.... I expect very little in terms of the enrichment of humans' spiritual treasure from those who, out of mental laziness, superficiality, an over-scientific approach or whatever, have distanced themselves from the grand, eternal concerns of the heart. I expect nothing from those who say: "You shouldn't be thinking about that!" I expect even less from those who believe in a Heaven and a Hell just like the one we believed in as children, and I expect less still from those who claim, with all the seriousness of the fool, "All this is nothing but myths and fables; when people die they are buried, and that's that". I only have hopes for those who do not know, but who do not resign themselves to not knowing; those who will fight ceaselessly for the truth, placing their lives in the very struggle itself rather than in the victory'.

Buddhist novices debating in Dharamsala, India

Some pilgrimages have a cathedral or a mosque as their objective. Others lead to the heights of a mountain peak. But can sacredness be found on an altar, inside a pagoda or at the top of the cliff? Perhaps when pilgrims reach these objectives, they can't decide whether to gaze at the altar or to look out at the sea beyond, or across the rolling plains. Perhaps they can't decide whether to look within or without. Or perhaps they have to half-close their eyes in order to make out the objective of their pilgrimage, given its very interiority. These photographs of temples, pagodas and monasteries at the top of cliffs suggest all this and much more.

Convergences and divergences

Some particularly stunning photographs show weapons of death and destruction in settings which, we would suppose (since they have been designed for prayer), should be for the purpose of life. It is not easy to overcome the conflicts that exist within each religion and between different ones. Will religions ever be able to coexist, to be self-critical and allow themselves to transform mutually? It is a fact that for some time now movements encouraging inter-religious encounters have been making progress, though it is also true that these encounters are obstructed by reticence, rejection and difficulties within the very religions themselves.

And where does this reluctance to enter into inter-religious encounters or dialogues come from? Perhaps from a fear of loss, or of the weakening of our own identity (or rather, what we imagine to be our own identity)?

Can religions cooperate in order to allow for their coexistence in the world? And if so, how? Can and should religions aim to facilitate harmony between humans and nations? Certainly it will be no easy matter to bring about a situation in which religions help to replace spiralling violence with peace processes.

Can religions contribute towards world coexistence by jointly promoting peace processes and the end of violence of all kinds? Admittedly, for some time inter-religious efforts have been made to promote world peace, though it is also true that there has been criticism from outside the religions, opposed to their roles in peace processes. And who is it that rejects the role of religions in promoting peace? Sometimes it comes from the belligerent propaganda, or even politics, of certain people or groups that use religion for ideological ends. There are others who think that world peace can only be built on exclusively secular foundations, since they believe that religions – once they go beyond the private sphere of citizens – are inherently propagandistic and aggressive.

If the people from the different religions portrayed in these photographs in an attitude of prayer were to meet around a table, could they come to an agreement? It would be easy to begin by getting to know each other and finding out what they had in common. By sitting together and conversing, they could develop sufficient trust to begin talking about their differences, which would serve as a stimulus for their mutual transformation. But before entering into dialogue of any depth, each spirituality or religion would need to be able to carry out a public self-criticism, by acknowledging the burden of history, the centuries of wealth and penury, and even, sometimes, the betrayal of the very founding traditions of the faiths. Through these three steps (which cannot be achieved in a single day, nor even in a month), people could begin to build a common horizon of language and dialogue, allowing each one to transform itself without forcibly or syncretistically inventing a kind of Esperanto of religions. Finally, this process would be incomplete without a profound sharing of the elements that could be called (providing the word is not misinterpreted) mystical. And not just sharing action or dialogue, but also silence: being able to commune in contemplative quiet, so that the mystery that penetrates, surrounds and overflows from every religion leads to a spirituality that exists beyond all of them.

Utopias of peace and realities of violence

But isn't this all just a Utopian dream? Doesn't history serve to undermine the house of cards of peaceful, spiritual coexistence? While the countenance of the meditating lama might proclaim tranquillity, the face of the furious preacher stirs up aggression. As we look through these photographs, we recall episodes in history (such as the St Bartholomew's Day massacre in 16th-century France, or the looting of Rome) that were all undertaken 'in the name of a god'.

In the name of what god did those people commit suicide in Waco, Texas, in 1993? In the name of what gospel did the ministers in the Ivory Coast allegedly recommend to the president Simone Gbagbo that she send out death squads to eliminate the Muslim ethnic groups in the north of the country? In the name of what god can one attempt to justify the mutual massacres of Hutus and Tutsis in Rwanda? In the name of what divinity did Saddam Hussein justify the invasion of Kuwait, George Bush the invasion of Iraq and Bush Jr the invasions of Afghanistan and Iraq? In the name of which god did the Japanese kamikaze aeroplanes take off in the war in the Pacific, or the planes smash into the Twin Towers in New York in 2001? In the name of which god did Gideon (as well as many any other men of war who appear in the Bible) fight to take possession of a land that God had presumably promised to a chosen people? When Christianity ceased to be persecuted in Rome and became the religion of the Empire, in the name of what kind of credo did the Christians, in turn, become the persecutors, and sow their prejudices against the Jews? Beneath what holy standard was the First Crusade organized in 1096? Rome made Augustus a divine being, just as Japan did with their Emperor. A dollar bill bears the words: 'In God we trust'. In Britain they sing 'God save the Queen'. In Spain, under Franco's National Catholicism, they used to proclaim, 'For God, the Motherland and the King' and, 'For the Empire toward God'. What kind of god, gods or idols are we talking about with respect to actions such as these?

These are just a few examples, which I have abbreviated to save the reader from having to plough through an interminable list of killings of heretics and witch hunts. Even the supposedly peaceful Buddhism is not excluded from this list – while Buddhist teachings encourage non-violence, martial arts originated in monasteries, and are still taught and practised there.

I began thinking a lot about these subjects after I took part in an inter-religious study conference with Doctor Yoshiharu Tomatsu, a Buddhist monk from the Jodo Shu branch and a professor at Taisho University, in Tokyo. He told me that in the Buddhist tradition, which dates back to Shakamuni, the main practices taught are non-violence, not harming anyone, and pacifying yourself and the society around you. Neither in the most ancient sacred writings in the Pali language, nor in the texts subsequently collected during Mayan Buddhism, can any justification for violence be found. Nevertheless, violence can unfortunately be found throughout the history of Asia.

The most commonly quoted words of the Buddha, in which he preaches non-violence, can be found in the *Dhammapada*, one of the oldest of the *sutra* texts in the Pali language: 'In this world, hatred can never be pacified with hatred. Hatred can only be vanquished by non-violence. This is an eternal law' [I, 5]. In fact, this is one of the texts often quoted by Buddhist groups in America following the September 11 attacks, in a call for peace and reconciliation. Among the many other texts that we could quote here, one of the most memorable is from the *Brahma Net Sutra*, from Mayan Buddhism, which says: 'A disciple of Buddha should not return hatred for hatred, blow for blow. He should not avenge himself, not even on those who kill his father, his mother, his sons, his daughters or his relatives. Not even if they murder the leader of his country. Taking one life to avenge another goes against filial piety, given that all lives are interconnected' [VI, 21].

But the same people who quote these texts acknowledge that Buddhists, just like Jews, Christians and Muslims, have contradicted and betrayed their religious traditions during the course of history. It is well known that Japanese Buddhists supported their government's militarism in the war in the Pacific, for example. Members of Sri Lanka's Buddhist community also supported their country's government in its civil war against the Tamil minority. Myanmar, an extremely Buddhist society, seems to be unable to rid itself of the oppression of its dictatorial government. These are just a few examples, and if we look back through history, we can easily find others.

After a Christian at the conference had carried out a self-criticism of the Crusades and the Inquisition, Professor Tomatsu referred to an interesting episode in Buddhist history that is set down in the *Mahavamsa* chronicles, from Teravada Buddhism, in the south of Sri Lanka. King Duttagamani was leading his forces into battle against an Indian kingdom; his army brandished a standard with the relics of Buddha as they charged, and there were even monks enlisted in his force. But when he saw the extent of the killing, the king was wracked by remorse. However, a group of monks promptly absolved him, calming him with a theological explanation justifying the massacre. They told him that as their enemies were not Buddhist believers, they could be considered no better than animals. This reminded me of Sepúlveda's argument against Las Casas, when he tried to justify the way that the colonizing Spaniards had treated the natives: he quoted a text from Aristotle which claims that some beings are slaves by their very nature. I would not have dared to mention the case of the Sri Lankan king before my Buddhist companions, out of tactfulness, but it was Professor Tomatsu – one of them – who mentioned it, by way of self-criticism. Later on he added that the importance of the passage lay in the fact that it had recently been used by fundamentalists in Sri Lanka to justify the central government's stance against the Tamil forces. This defence is similar, he said, to the one used by the Japanese Buddhists in the war in the Pacific to justify the actions of the government's Shintoist ideology, under the pretext of protecting the family, the nation and the Emperor.

Meanwhile, there is a text in the Mayan school version of the *Mahaparinirvana Sutra* which goes so far as to claim that it is acceptable to kill someone in order to save the lives of many more [XII, 19]. Those who attempted to justify the atom bomb or, more recently, the preventive war against Iraq, made use of similar pseudo-religious justifications. Listening to Professor Tomatsu talking about National Shintoism, I could not help but think of National Catholicism in Spain, with its patriotic-religious slogans.

Some Buddhists who recognize this incoherence in their own religion have reinterpreted the aforementioned texts in a different way. In his 1993 book *For a Future to be Possible: Commentaries on the Five Wonderful Precepts*, the Vietnamese Buddhist monk and peace activist Thich Nhat Hanh reinterprets the first Buddhist commandment 'Do not kill' in the following way: 'Being aware of the suffering caused by the destruction of life, I promise to cultivate compassion and to learn to protect the lives of people, animals, plants and minerals'. That's all very well, but will fanatics and fundamentalists pay him any heed?

Does faith engender violence?

Yet there is one serious potential obstacle to the coexistence of different forms of spirituality and the contribution that religions can make to global harmony: don't religions, by their very nature, tend towards intolerance? Isn't that what history – and even neurology – shows us? This is how the situation is presented in *What Makes Us Think? A Neuroscientist and a Philosopher Argue About Ethics, Human Nature, and the Brain*, an intellectual conversation between the neuroscientist Jean-Pierre Changeux and the hermeneutist Paul Ricoeur. In the final paragraphs devoted to universal ethics and cultural conflicts, the two men discuss the subject of violence and religion. In response to Changeux's criticism that religions possess a violent factor, Ricoeur admits that a problem exists in the very heart of the phenomenon of religion: the relationship between conviction and violence that is accentuated when the cultural fact of unilaterality is combined with the affirmation of identity. How is it possible, Changeux asks, for us to aspire to a global system of ethics in the middle of a world dominated by cultural, political and religious conflicts? Shouldn't the construction of an ethical project beyond cultural and religious differences necessarily be carried out by secular means? Don't religions divide more than they unite?

Ricoeur attempted to highlight the triumph of something more profound in the phenomenon of religion: the radical trust that gives meaning and which precedes the possibility of mutually trusting in the word divorced from dialogue. But the French hermeneutist recognizes that limits exist: we cannot converse with several cultures and religions at the same depth in the same way that we cannot have many close friends at the same time. But even so, Ricoeur does not profess to have a neutral posture when judging different religions and cultures. He proposes a dual process, first and foremost acknowledging the limited nature of viewpoint itself (which can never be overcome), and second attempting to place oneself in the position of the person with whom one is speaking (though this can never be achieved completely). If both parties carry out this dual recognition, it gradually becomes possible to widen the fusion of horizons within the dialogue. To make an analogue with language, it's not the same for someone who has been bilingual from birth as someone who learns a second language as an adult, using the left-hand side of their brain. Such limitations exist in inter-religious intercultural dialogues when we attempt to develop (without ever completely achieving it) a kind of cultural and religious bilingualism.

Changeux, however, insists on the existence of a link – even at a neurological level – between religion and intolerance, one which unfortunately has been confirmed by history. This idea cannot easily be ruled out, and Ricoeur acknowledges it honestly and attempts to rebut it using his own religiosity. 'I find myself,' he said in *De l'interpretation, Du Seuil*, published in 1965, 'in a situation that can be expressed by a geometrical comparison of the surface of a sphere. If I attempt to cover it eclectically, I will never discover the universal; furthermore, I will end up in syncretism. But if I go deeper into my tradition, I can begin to go beyond the limits of language itself. Thus I can move toward the centre of the sphere, toward the dimension of profoundness, while other people continue to travel the surface, meeting up or disagreeing and separating. Huge distances on the surface become shorter if we travel to the centre to find ourselves there.'

Ricoeur continues: 'It is specifically in the depths of that centre that I discover that other convictions exist that are different to mine. Tolerance is not imposed upon me from above, telling me not to leave my part of the sphere. I discover it from within, when I go deeper into my own place and travel along the radius to the centre of the sphere. It is then that I realize that religiousness is, in itself, pluralism and fragmentation. Religiosity does not only exceed its own expressions, it inhabits other people and other cultures in a different way to the way in which it inhabits me; it is not exclusive to my religion, it takes place in other religions, also, and even in contemporary non-religious society.'

If the photos in this collection represent a testimony to anything, it is precisely that pluralism and fragmentation of the religious experience.

In the name of 'no god'?

This introduction, which I wrote at the end of the editing process, may seem more like an epilogue than a foreword. The original intention was to leave the photographs to pose the questions themselves. They present the ambiguity – the mixture of good and evil, peacemaking and violence – that permeates the history of religions. At the end of the journey, there is an unknown factor: will we have to achieve a pacified and pacifying spirituality in the future 'in the name of "no god"'? Will we have to get rid of religion in order to rediscover spirituality, to endure that dark night of crisis of religions so that dawn can break once again on religiosity? If we want to overcome violence and live together in peace, don't we need a meeting of religions that goes beyond mere dialogue, and a transformation of spirituality that goes beyond religions? Do spirituality and religiosity have a future? I hope they do, but only on the condition that they desist from making any absolute claims on sacredness, and that they do not take in vain the name of any god made idol.

After centuries of many, many words, there should be silence. When Bodhidharma arrived in China in the 6th century, he disconcerted the Emperor (a devout Buddhist) by the way he answered a question on the essence of Buddhism. 'Everything can be reduced to an enormous Void', said the patriarch. The monarch was perplexed. The monk, meanwhile, postponed his missionary project and withdrew into solitude. It is there, legend has it, that he spent long years engaged in meditation, attempting to empty himself and to submerge himself in the Void.

But theoretical silence is compatible with the liberating practice of suffering. Siddharta Gautama became disheartened by the sterility of the debate. Seeing a man wounded by an

The Hare Krishna Festival of Janmashtami in the temple at Bhaktivedanta Manor, Hertfordshire, England.

arrow, he said: 'Don't waste time trying to find out who shot it. Just try to heal the wound'. On another occasion, the Master said to a governor: 'Do you have an expert accountant who can calculate how many grains of sand there are in the desert? That is how unfathomable the ultimate mystery of reality is'. To the monarch's surprise, the monk continues by asking, 'Where does the flame go after the fire is put out?' To name this ultimate secret of reality (*Tathâgata*, in Sanskrit), neither affirmations nor negations can be used; saying 'it exists' is just the same as saying 'it does not exist'. That is why Zen offers so many enigmas (*koans*) in order to break with man's slavery to logic: 'The monk asked the Master Pei-shu: "What is the Buddha?" The Master answered: "A cat climbing a column". "I don't understand", replied the monk. "Ask the column", said the Master'.

Vindication of silence

In conclusion, no more explanatory details. Don't touch it, that's just the way the rose is. Let us remain puzzled before the ambivalence of sacredness, and pass from perplexity to silence. The Zen masters tell us that we should empty our ego and leave our selves. These remarks by the Master Dogen say more than many other interpretations: 'Achieving enlightenment is like the reflection of the moon on the water. The moon does not get wet, nor does the sheet of water become broken. Great is the moon and wide is the radius of its rays of light, but everything fits in a drop of water. The entire moon and all the sky are contained and reflected in each drop of dew.' A drop of water reflects the whole of the moon; at nightfall, in the West and in the East, the same moon can be seen. The Whole exists in each place and moment, if one has eyes to see it. Nothing is profane, said Teilhard de Chardin, for he who knows how to look. But if the drop of water insists on being nothing but a drop, it will not reflect the moon.

'If you meet the Buddha, kill him', says the master, the *Rôshi*. The 16th-century priest and poet John of the Cross would have understood. It is not a negation of God, but rather a rejection of all anthropomorphism and idolatry. Though popular religiosity calls for images, to a great extent the iconoclasts were right.

The Western thinker has to give up two forms of idolatry: those of argued reason and clear reason, both of which are closely linked to the desire for individualism. We cling to the former (in philosophy) out of a fear of the irrationality of the emotional-imaginative-narrative world. We cling onto the latter (in theology) out of a fear of pantheism. As a result, we are imprisoned in the jail of rationalist and dualist thinking. That is why we must first destroy the idols to rediscover the symbols. The Pseudo-Dionysius the Areopagite wrote in his *Letter to Gaius*: 'if anyone sees God and recognizes what he is seeing, then he hasn't seen God himself'. Panikkar comments: 'Could an atheist religion ever exist? The Buddha's answer is categorical: the only real religion is one that is atheist; anything else is simple idolatry, the worshipping of a God, the work of our hands and our minds'.

The patriarch Dogen insisted on the obviousness of the absolute, far-away and near, familiar and impalpable. He returned from China with not much luggage, but with wisdom in his veins. He summarized his learning by saying: 'The line of the nose is vertical, and the line of the eyes is horizontal'. By this, he was encouraging others to seek the profound in what was immediately present, the absolute in the relative and the divine in the everyday.

'Anyone who plants a palm tree will never eat its dates', they say in the southwest of Spain; it is the next generation who enjoy the fruit. In the West, one typical example is the anonymity of the men who build cathedrals. In the East, one's attention is caught by those pagodas in which architectural miracles have been achieved without using one single nail; simply by assembling pieces of wood. The wood came from very old trees, and was cut and prepared well: the pagodas are the result of an inestimable amount of time and silent anonymous efforts.

You cannot make a plant grow faster by pulling it upwards – all you will succeed in doing is uprooting it. All living organisms have their own rhythm. Taoism captured the essence of this idea by tuning into the Tao – the Way that rules everything harmoniously. It allows everything to follow its natural course, leave itself, live in communion with nature and perceive the Way in the heart of that which is slow, everyday and silent.

One popular Zen saying goes: 'Don't paint feet on the snake'. The snake is the easiest animal to paint for nursery school children – all you need to do is paint a curving line with the paintbrush. But grown-ups tend to ruin the picture by adding details, and the snake is thus turned into a centipede.

Once a beginner was trying hard to meditate, but the master told him off: 'Forget yourself and stop thinking!' he said. 'With the path that you're travelling, you'll never reach enlightenment.' When the disciple thought he had achieved his goal, he was very pleased with himself; it seemed to him as though he could feel the presence of Buddha himself at his side. But he was wracked by doubt: 'If I turn the corner and I meet Buddha, what shall I say to him?' He wasn't expecting the master's reply: 'If you are walking along and you meet Buddha in person, don't hesitate to kill him'. The disciple was disconcerted, and he took a while to understand: he could and should kill him because, if he appeared in this way, then he definitely wasn't Buddha but merely a hallucination.

In the West, it is difficult to come to terms with this form of spirituality, which is so heavily based on suggestion without any explicit explanations. It is like the tale of the atheist who challenged God by saying: 'If you exist, make the bird perched on that branch fly towards me'. After a while, the bird flew off in the opposite direction. The atheist began trembling: 'Now I see that you do exist', he said. Just another example of Buddhist suggestion, for if the bird had fulfilled the atheist's wishes, it would not have proved that God existed, but rather that it was an idol that could be controlled by anyone, in order to use it 'in the name of a god'.

We Westerners have inherited from Ancient Greece the art of thinking aloud. In the East, they think while they breathe. One breathes when seated, like the Buddha in meditation. Rodin's *Thinker* tenses himself in order to think, while the Buddha in contemplation stretches out so as not to think, and relaxes in order to breathe properly. From that non-thinking and that silent breathing comes a form of thinking that is dense, concise and mature; it is the result of sitting down to listen after having walked for a while, and then getting up to walk again after having listened. Just like in the biblical tradition: listen as you walk and walk as you listen.

Western spirituality and religiosity, being the heirs of a verbalizing tradition, will need strong doses of silence and slow breathing to discover the new spirituality beyond religious forms. Instead of creating a new kind of preaching, we will have to go in search of a new silence. The culture of breathing may help us to cultivate our sensibility toward the spirit that blows where and how it wishes.

When Pope John Paul II visited Nagasaki, it was snowing. The purplish red of the cardinals' sashes together with the white of the pontiff's robes, set against the whiteness of the snow, strongly evoked the Japanese flag. The climax of a day charged with emotion was when everyone knelt down to pray for peace, remembering the victims of the atomic bomb. It was, therefore, tempting for television cameras to focus in on scenes such as when the eyes of the old Pope began to water from the emotion and the cold. However, one Japanese director had the intuitive idea of fading the shot by putting it out of focus. Western minds assumed this was a mistake by the cameramen, but the artistic photographer defended his decision: 'Too much light reflecting from the snow and too much attention on the Pope's face. It was better to fade both, filtering the light and relaxing the tension. A little more half-light and serenity fit in with the spiritual climate of the scene better.'

Something similar happened when a group of Japanese monks visited some European monasteries. On their return to Japan, they remarked: 'Why are there so many images of saints, in the cloisters and on the altarpieces, all praying with their hands tightly, tensely clasped, while rays of celestial light

Tiny offerings in the form of coloured ribbons for the victims of the atom bomb at the Peace Memorial Park in Hiroshima, Japan

descend upon them? Wouldn't it be more appropriate for them to be praying with their hands spread out or placed together without the tension and in a setting of more half-light?'

When considering these anecdotes together with the photographs in this collection, I have only one thing to say: no comment.

JUAN MASIÁ CLAVEL
Lecturer at the Faculty of Theology,
Sophia University, Tokyo

PILGRIMAGES

According to the Latin etymology of the word, a pilgrim is someone who travels through fields (*per agra*); they pass through lands as a foreigner or a stranger. But in many religions, since ancient times, the pilgrim has been clearly distinguished from the vagabond or the simple traveller. Pilgrimages have spiritual motivations and objectives, even today when the behaviour, clothing and lifestyles of these 'walking seekers' often make them look like tourists or hikers.

The old Roman Catholic catechism used to list one of the works of mercy as giving lodging to pilgrims, in accordance with the biblical tradition of hospitality. But hospitality is a word with unstable origins. 'Hospitality', 'hospice' and 'hospital' all derive from the Latin word *hostes*, which can mean either 'guest' or 'host'. But if we change one letter – the 'e' for an 'i' – then 'guest' becomes 'enemy' – *hostis* in Latin. The traveller who asks for lodging may be a friend or an enemy; he may arouse hospitality or hostility. Isn't that just what happens with religious pilgrimages, which can be either a collective symbol of a peaceful community or a warlike revolt? Perhaps one should always ask pilgrims why they are walking, and what their objective is.

In fact, the metaphor of the path is one of the most important of the symbols leading to the mystery of sacredness. Buddhism is the way of enlightenment. Confucianism is the way of harmony in human relations. Taoism is the return to the primordial unity of the Way. Shintoism bears this name because it is the way of the *kami*, or divinities. All Muslims are obliged to travel the way to Mecca, at least once in their lives. The community of John the Baptist placed in Christ's mouth the confession of identity: 'I am the Way'; and in Antioch, before the followers of Jesus came to be called Christians, they were known as 'the people of the Way'.

Religious processions, though they are not without their ambiguities, manifest a search for holiness on a popular level. But sometimes it is just a small step from a procession to a riot, from a gathering of the faithful to a revolt of the masses. That is what

Poland *Pilgrimage to the Black Virgin of Czestochowa*

happened in Ephesus, when the silversmiths rebelled against Paul. The people who bought the smiths' objects to offer at the temple (in the process affording them lucrative earnings) were manipulated, whipped up, by the traders – and what began as a procession to a temple of Diana ended up as a demonstration against Paul. Luke describes it graphically: 'Everyone was shouting something, because they were excited, while the others did not know why everyone had come together' [Acts, 19:32]. Whether alone or in groups, members of the faithful from the most diverse beliefs – as well as people without any particular belief but who are in some way seeking meaning, identity or hope – all travel the routes of the pagodas and relics of Buddha in India and Sri Lanka, or the road to Santiago, or the path that leads to Mecca, or the route that passes through the 88 Buddhist sanctuaries on the Japanese island of Shikoku. Is there a common objective in all these pilgrimages?

There is no divergence in the words of the Buddhas,
There is no more than one single vehicle, not two.
Countless Buddhas crossed
The threshold of that nirvana in the past;
During infinite centuries, incalculable is their number.
So blessed,
With opportune resources and appropriate parables,
They preached in each case
The variety of faces
Of one single teaching.
They all proclaimed
The Dharma of the one Vehicle;
They taught many beings,
And they introduced them to the way of the Buddha.
Knowing well as they did the human heart,
They served as resources and aid
To reveal the Primordial.

LOTUS SUTRA, CHAPTER I

27 *Sanctuary of Fátima, Portugal* • 28–9 *Pushkar, India* • 30–31 *Sanctuary of Lourdes, France*
Opposite *Medjugorje, Bosnia and Herzegovina* • Above *Maha Kumbh Mela, India*

33

Above *Mecca, Saudi Arabia* • 36–7 *Almonte, Spain* • 38–9 *Antigua Guatemala, Guatemala* • 40–41 *Lhasa, Tibet*

Above *Lalibela, Ethiopia* • Opposite *Sanctuary of Lourdes, France* • 44 *Salvador de Bahía, Brazil* • 45 *Mashad, Iran* • 46 *Our Lady of Luján, Argentina*
47 *Santiago de Compostela, Spain* • 48–9 *Golden Temple, Amritsar, India* • 50–51 *Czestochowa, Poland* • 52–3 *Aswan, Egypt*

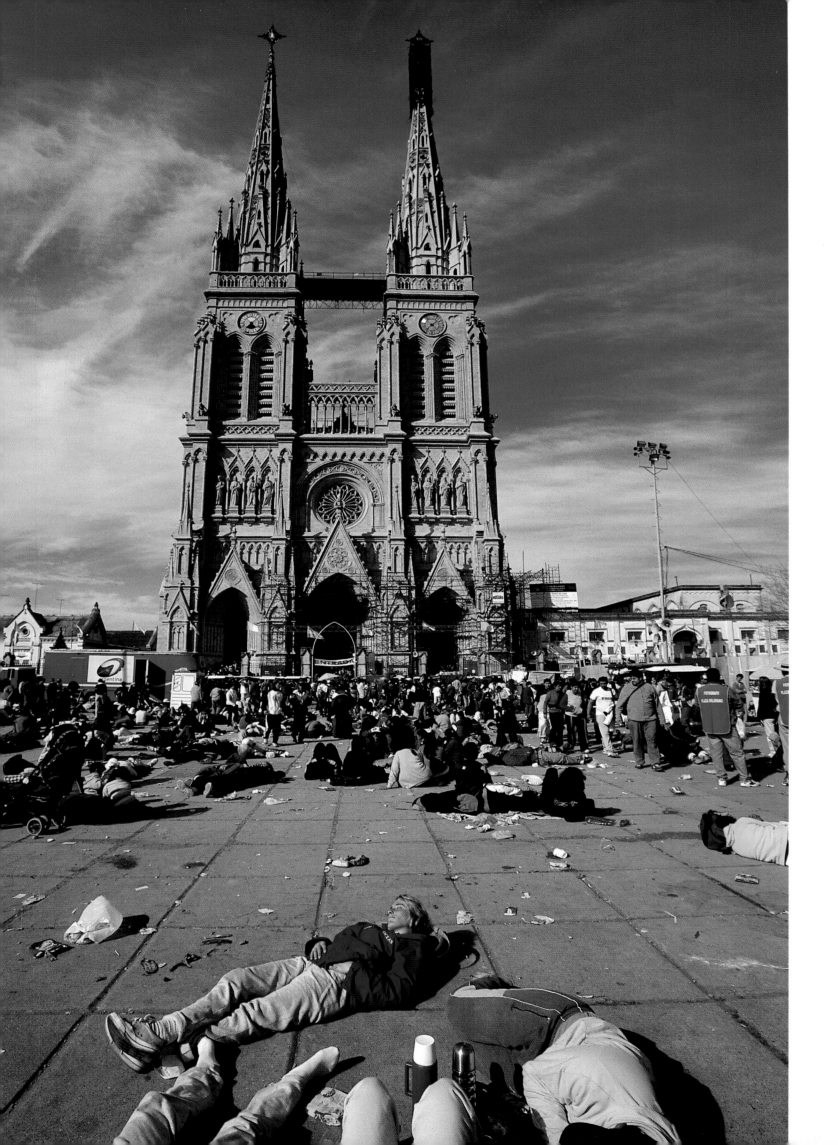

27 Sanctuary of Fátima, Portugal

Every year on 13 May, a vast pilgrimage commemorates the anniversary of the apparition of the Virgin to three shepherds in the cave of Iria in 1917. The Virgin called for a chapel to be built, which was the origin of the present-day sanctuary; she also predicted the end of the First World War and the premature deaths of two of the shepherds. All of her predictions came true.

28–9 Pushkar, India

In the holy city of Pushkar, the birthplace of Brahma, god of creation, the consumption of meat, eggs and alcohol is prohibited. Thousands of Hindu pilgrims travel here to pray in the city's temples and bathe in the ghats of its sacred lake.

30–31 Sanctuary of Lourdes, France

In 1858, a poor, illiterate 12-year-old girl called Bernadette Soubirous claimed she had seen the Virgin Mary in a small cave on no fewer than 18 occasions. In 1862, the Catholic Church approved the apparitions, and in 1933 Bernadette was canonized. Every year, six million pilgrims come to the sanctuary in the hope of a miracle.

32 Medjugorje, Bosnia and Herzegovina

On 24 June 1981, in a small village near the Croat border in present-day Bosnia and Herzegovina, the Virgin appeared before six young people and revealed ten 'secrets'. The Catholic Church has not yet made a declaration on the event's supernatural nature.

33 Maha Kumbh Mela, India

Every twelve years, when the planets and other celestial bodies are aligned, the Maha Kumbh Mela is celebrated in Haridwar, a holy site for Hindus and the point where the sacred Ganges, Yamuna and Saraswati rivers converge. The forces of creation come together in a receptacle (Kumbh), thereby generating a celebration (Mela). It is the most multitudinous religious event in the world; in February 2001, some 13 million people attended.

34 Our Lady of Guadalupe, Mexico City, Mexico

The sanctuary of Our Lady of Guadalupe, on Tepeyac hill, is the most visited pilgrimage site in the Western world. Every 12 December, pilgrims commemorate the day when the Virgin appeared before a peasant in 1531. The event was particularly momentous since it led to the conversion to Christianity of millions of indigenous people.

35 Mecca, Saudi Arabia

Pilgrimages to Mecca are usually undertaken in the month of Dhul-Hijjah, and last for five days. During this time, pilgrims visit the al-Haram Mosque, circle the Kaaba (visible in the centre of this photograph) with its Black Stone, drink water from the well of Zamzam and visit the town of Mina.

36–7 Almonte, Spain

The origin of the romería (pilgrimage) of Rocío dates back to the times of King Alfonso X (the Wise). A million people gather together at the village after several days of travelling, in an event that mixes faith and folklore. The key moment comes when the pilgrims leap the railings of the hermitage and bring out, shoulder high, the Virgin Mary – the 'white dove'.

38–9 Antigua Guatemala, Guatemala

Easter week in Antigua is without any doubt the most important traditional and religious event in Guatemala. Thousands of visitors arrive in the city which, with over 450 years of history, is imbued with an atmosphere of great spirituality for several days.

40–41 Lhasa, Tibet

In the capital of Tibet stands Potala Palace, the winter residence of the Dalai Lama since the 7th century. The stunning complex of chapels, administrative buildings and monastery is the largest construction in Tibet.

42 Lalibela, Ethiopia

The masterpiece of the holy city of Lalibela is the monolithic church of St George, 11 metres (36 feet) high and carved out of granite. It has been a site of pilgrimage for Coptic Christians since the 8th century.

43 Sanctuary of Lourdes, France

The Grotto of the Revelations of Mary. More than 300 employees, around 30 priests and several religious communities cater to the needs of six million pilgrims every year. The sanctuary's large budget comes from donations.

44 Salvador de Bahía, Brazil

The procession of Nosso Senhor do Bonfim – Our Lord of the Good End – which mixes Catholic and animist faiths, sets off from the church of Our Lady of the Conception and, after much dancing, praying and singing, arrives at the church of Bonfim. Once it has arrived at the church, the religious syncretism becomes even more apparent, with washing rites and praising of Nosso Senhor taking place alongside the worship of Oxalá, the most important deity of the Candomblé gods.

45 Mashad, Iran

The Mausoleum of Ali ibn Musa al-Rida, the 8th Shi'ite Iman (a descendant of the Prophet Muhammad who was poisoned by the Caliph Ma'mun in 818) is the most important Shi'ite pilgrimage site in Iran. Millions of people visit the site every year.

46 Our Lady of Luján, Argentina

In the first week of October every year thousands of people set off from the church of Liniers in Buenos Aires on a long pilgrimage to the Gothic basilica of Our Lady of Luján, the patron saint of Argentina.

47 Santiago de Compostela, Spain

In Obradoiro Square stands the cathedral where the relics of St James the Apostle (Santiago) are worshipped. Together with Jerusalem and Rome, the city is one of the most important sites in Christianity.

48–9 Golden Temple, Amritsar, India

The Golden Temple is the most sacred site for Sikhs, and is also whereFuru Nanak, the first master of Sikhism.

50–51 Czestochowa, Poland

This sanctuary is the home of an image of the Black Virgin which, according to legend, was painted by St Luke on the wooden table of the Holy Family, and then taken to Constantinople. Centuries later, following a victory over the Tartars, a Polish prince brought the image to Czestochowa, where it has since become famous for working miracles.

52–3 Aswan, Egypt

If their health and finances allow, every Muslim is obliged to travel at least once in their life to Mecca. The journey, which can last several months, is a great event, and on their return, pictures are painted on the walls of the pilgrims' houses testifying to their holy voyage.

DWELLINGS OF HOLINESS

Temples, sanctuaries, pagodas, mosques, monasteries, cathedrals, basilicas, chapels, meditation rooms at airports and hermitages...are they all equally holy places? Are they all spaces that can reveal the elusive presence of the divine? And do such rich decorations constitute symbolic offerings, or are they merely reflections of the power that sponsored their construction? And the stones of the cathedrals and the pyramids – are they engraved with the marks of piety, or the blood and sweat of the human labour that built those pillars? Are they places of gratitude or of sacrifice?

Temples and similar places that offer the chance of an encounter with holiness are viewed in different cultures as spaces where one can come into contact with the world of the transcendental. That is why they have been given names such as 'House of Divinity', or 'House of Prayer'. But the history of religion includes examples of attempts to prevent the degeneration of dwellings of holiness into centres of power. The Gospels tell how Jesus criticized the Temple, calling it a 'cave of bandits' [Mark, 15:17] and a 'house of business' [John 2:16]. And today, what should we call Fátima, Lourdes or the Basilica of St Peter in Rome? Are they tourist centres or places of prayer? Areas of miracles or of spectacles? The dwellings of holiness or an escape from reality?

Iran *Friday prayers, Tehran University*

Ethiopia *The Coptic church of Lalibela*

Surely there is a vein for the silver,
And a place for gold where they find it.
Iron is taken out of the earth,
And brass is molten out of the stone.

As for the earth, out of it cometh bread:
And under it is turned up as it were fire.
The stones of it are the place of sapphires:
And it hath dust of gold.

Man putteth forth his hand upon the rock;
He overturneth the mountains by the roots.
He cutteth out rivers among the rocks;
And his eye seeth every precious thing.
He bindeth the floods from overflowing;
And the thing that is hid bringeth he forth
    to light.

But where shall wisdom be found?
And where is the place of understanding?

BOOK OF JOB, 28:1–12

58–9 *Pyramids of Giza, Cairo, Egypt* • 60–61 *Abu Simbel, Egypt* • 62–3 *Polonnaruwa, Sri Lanka* • 64–5 *Yangon, Myanmar*
66 *Aksum, Ethiopia* • 67 *Mount Emei, Sichuan Province, China* • Opposite *Lalibela, Ethiopia* • Above *Pak Ou Caves, Laos*

Above *Blue Mosque, Istanbul, Turkey*

Above *Western Wall, Jerusalem, Israel* • Opposite *Via Crucis, Jerusalem, Israel*

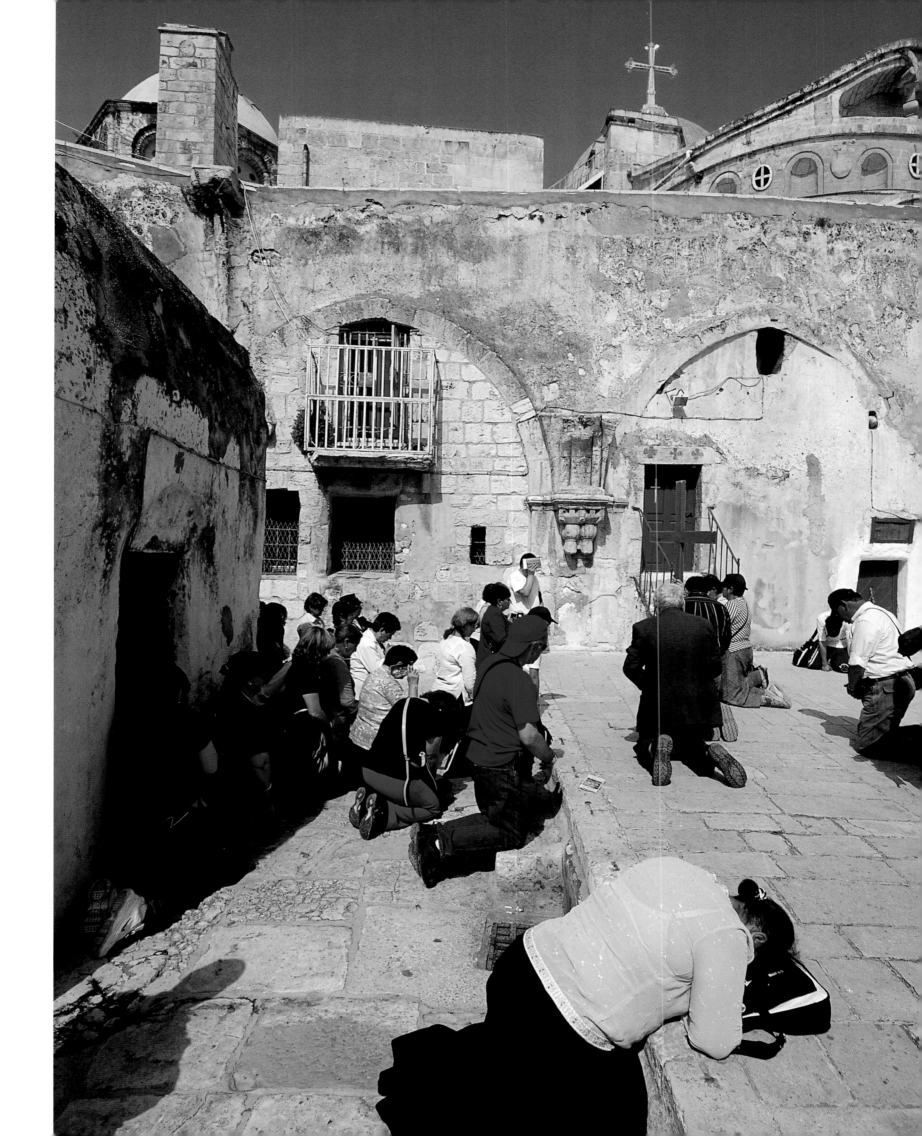

Above *Church of the Holy Sepulchre, Jerusalem, Israel*

Above *Ise Shrine, Mie Prefecture, Japan*

Above *Mausoleum of Ayatollah Khomeini, Tehran, Iran* • 92–3 *St Basil's Cathedral, Moscow, Russia* • 94–5 *Djingareyber Mosque, Timbuktu, Mali*

91

Opposite *Grand Mosque, Bobo Dioulasso, Burkina Faso* • Above *Great Mosque, Kairouan, Tunisia*
100–101 *Shwedagon Pagoda, Yangon, Myanmar* • 102 *San Andrés Xecul, Guatemala* • 103 *Ruwanweliseya Dagoba, Anuradhapura, Sri Lanka*

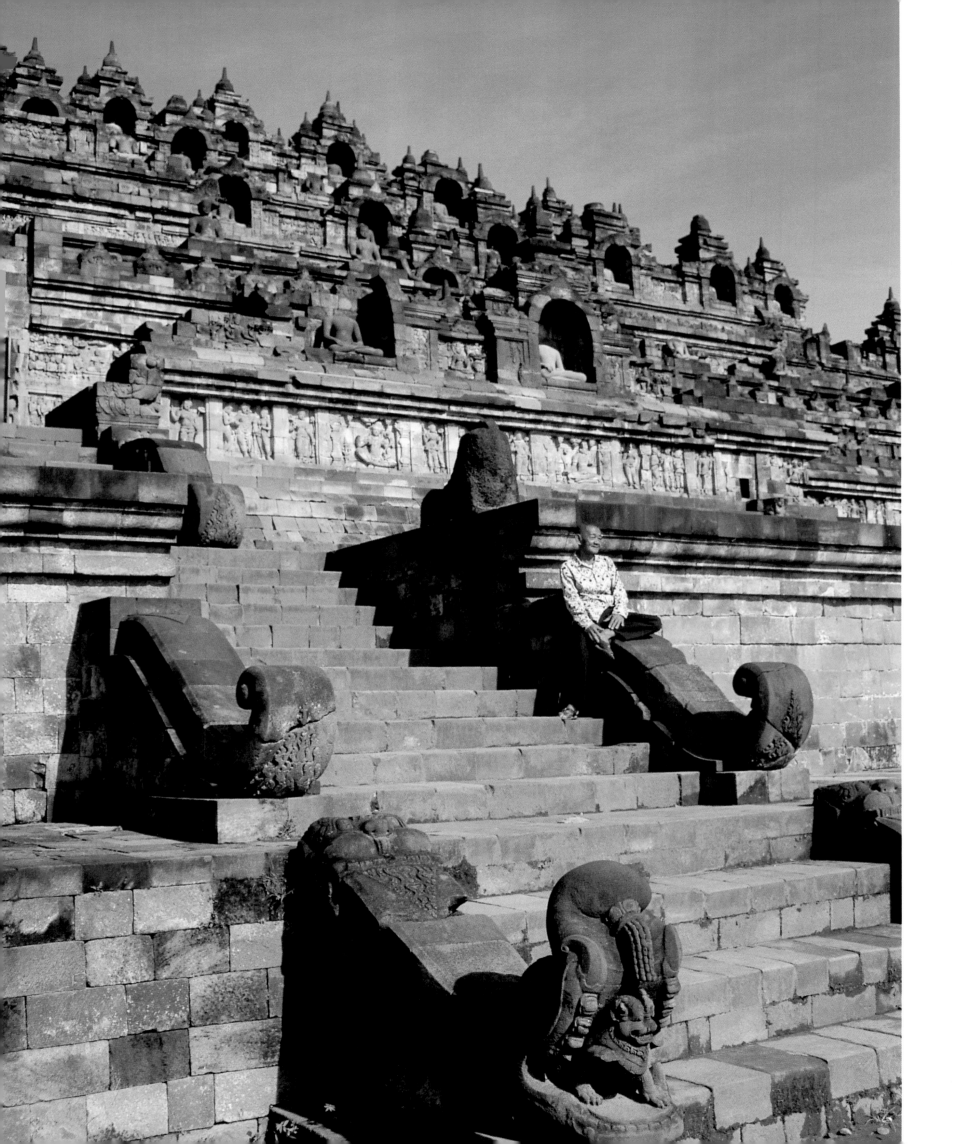

Opposite *Borobudur, Magelang, Java, Indonesia* • Above *Ladakh, India* • 106–107 *Tengboche Monastery, Nepal*

58–9 Pyramids of Giza, Cairo, Egypt

Built four-and-a-half millennia ago, the pyramids of Giza are the most visited monuments in Egypt, as well as being one of the wonders of humanity. Until the 19th century, the Great Pyramid at Giza, the tomb of the Pharaoh Cheops, was the tallest building in the world.

67 Mount Emei, Sichuan Province, China

On Mount Emei stands one of the most important holy statues in China, a stone Buddha some 71 metres (233 feet) high, carved in the 8th century. Today, however, this statue is danger – acid rain is damaging the surface, and part of its curls and one ear are at the point of falling off.

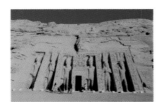

60–61 Abu Simbel, Egypt

Abu Simbel ('The sacred mountain') is a complex of two temples hewn out of solid rock by Rameses II and dedicated to the worship of the Pharaoh himself as well as to the deities Amon, Ra and Ptah. Owing to the construction of the Aswan Dam, the temple was relocated, stone by stone, to a safer place.

68 Lalibela, Ethiopia

Ethiopia has one of the oldest Christian congregations in Africa, going back hundreds of years. Today there are over 30 million Christians in the country, as well as 25 million Muslims and a community of Jewish origin, the falashas, who have lived there since the 14th century and who, legend has it, are descended from King Solomon.

62–3 Polonnaruwa, Sri Lanka

This reclining statue, some 14 metres (49 feet) long, represents the Buddha entering the state of nirvana and belongs to the group of Buddha figures of Gal Vihara, which possess great religious significance.

69 Pak Ou Caves, Laos

On the banks of the Mekong River, near the city of Luang Praban, lie the Caves of the 10,000 Buddhas, the holiest site in the country. Thousands of tiny statues are carved out of the rock, making the caves a unique pilgrimage site.

64–5 Yangon, Myanmar

The six-storey pagoda of Chaukhtatgyi contains a colossal image of the 'reclining Buddha'. The original image, donated by a merchant in 1907, was damaged by the weather and had to be demolished. This new one, which was completed in 1966 and paid for by private donations, is 65.85 metres (216 feet) long.

70 Blue Mosque, Istanbul, Turkey

Built between 1603 and 1617, the 'Blue Mosque' stands opposite Hagia Sophia, and is the only mosque in the city with six minarets. Located very close to the Topkapi Palace, it was decorated using 21,043 coloured tiles.

66 Aksum, Ethiopia

A woman praying at the door of the Church of Our Lady of Zion, which is said to contain the Ark of the Covenant, and where all the country's emperors were crowned. The city of Aksum is the religious capital of the Ethiopian Coptic Church, and is an important pilgrimage site.

71 Angkor, Cambodia

Angkor Wat is the largest archeological site in the world; however, in recent decades it has suffered from war, abandonment and looting. The towers symbolize the Meru mountain, axis of the world and home of the gods, according to Hinduism.

72–3 Jama Masjid, New Delhi, India

In the old part of the city stands the Jama Masjid (Friday Mosque), the largest mosque in India. There is room for more than 25,000 people in its great courtyard.

74–5 Blue Mosque, Istanbul, Turkey

The interior of the Blue Mosque is decorated with spectacular tiles, those of the upper stories being blue and giving the mosque its name. Much of the original coloured glass was a gift from the Venetian Republic. To the left is the minbar or pulpit, from which the imam leads prayers.

76–7 St Peter's Square, Vatican City

The Vatican City state, occupying less than one square kilometre and with fewer than 1,000 inhabitants, is the site of the Holy See, the most important institution in the Catholic Church. The apostle St Peter is buried in the basilica that bears his name.

78–9 Yamusukro, Ivory Coast

Félix Houphouët-Boigny, former president of Ivory Coast, made Yamusukro, the town of his birth, the country's capital in 1983, giving it luxurious infrastructures (though these are now usually empty). A devout Catholic, and in spite of the lack of interest in this religion in his country, the president built and financed (with his 'personal fortune') the basilica of Notre-Dame de la Paix. After being consecrated by Pope John Paul II, it was donated to the Vatican.

80–81 Great Mosque, Djenné, Mali

The city's Great Mosque, built in 1280 following King Koi Komboro's conversion to Islam, is made from mud, reeds and wood, and is the largest adobe structure in the world. Foreigners have been banned from entering since a film crew made an advert in the building featuring scantily dressed women.

82–3 Registan, Samarkand, Uzbekistan

In the centre of Samarkand, the point where the Silk Road crosses the Tea Road, stands the Registan. Built between the 15th and 17th centuries, it is the site of three Qur'anic schools – Ulugbek, Shir-Dor Madrassa and Tillya-Kari Madrassa.

84–5 Dome of the Rock, Jerusalem

On the Haram al-Sharif or Temple Mount, stands the al-Sakhra mosque, better known as the 'Dome of the Rock', one of Islam's most important holy sites. Inside the mosque is the rock from which Muhammad ascended to Heaven, accompanied by the Angel Gabriel.

86 Western Wall, Jerusalem, Israel

The Western Wall, also known as the Wailing Wall, is the last remaining vestige of the Temple of Solomon, which was destroyed by the Romans. The Jews pray in front of it in the belief that it is the most accessible holy site on earth. In their prayers, they mourn the destruction of the city and the dispersion of the Jewish people.

87 Via Crucis, Jerusalem, Israel

The Via Crucis, which traces Christ's route bearing the cross, can be followed all year round, but it is especially significant during Lent or on Friday evenings, when the Franciscans (the custodians of the Christian holy places since the 13th century) process along the streets of old Jerusalem.

88 Church of the Holy Sepulchre, Jerusalem, Israel

According to tradition this church was built on Golgotha, the place of Christ's crucifixion. It is a modest, simple place, and its ceremonies are carefully divided up between Orthodox Greek, Armenian, Coptic, Roman Catholic and Orthodox Christians, to avoid any friction between them – so much so that, in order to prevent disputes, since the Ottoman period the keys have been kept by a Muslim family.

89 Ise Shrine, Mie Prefecture, Japan

The Ise Shrine is unusual in that it is dismantled and rebuilt every twenty years, using trees from the surrounding area. Shintoism preaches great love for the elements of nature, and its architecture amply demonstrates this relationship with the natural environment.

90 Dargah, Ajmer, India

Women praying before the Dargah, the tomb of the Sufi saint Khwaja Moinuddin Chishti, who came from Persia and died in 1236. This is one of the most sacred places in the country for Muslim pilgrims.

91 Mausoleum of Ayatollah Khomeini, Tehran, Iran

Just south of the Iranian capital stands this mausoleum, one of the largest Islamic constructions of the modern age. Every day it is visited by hundreds of people who come here to pray.

92–3 St Basil's Cathedral, Moscow, Russia

While actually called the Cathedral of the Intercession of the Virgin on the Hill, this striking building is better known as St Basil's Cathedral. It was built in the 16th century by the Tsar Ivan the Terrible, and is comprised of nine chapels – each one dedicated to the saint on whose feast day the Tsar had won a battle – surrounding a central tower.

94–5 Djingareyber Mosque, Timbuktu, Mali

Timbuktu, the holy city founded by the Tuaregs in the 12th century as a trade centre for the caravans of the Sahara, has today virtually become a ghost city. The only features that have been conserved are a museum, a market and three of the oldest mosques in Africa, including this one.

96 León Cathedral, León, Spain

This cathedral dates back to the days of King Ordoño II who, in thanks to God following a great victory over the Moors, ceded his palace (which was built on the site of a 2nd-century Roman baths) so that a cathedral could be built there. Consecrated in 1073, it was enlarged in the Gothic style in the 13th century. Each of its 737 stained glass windows is unique.

97 Silos Monastery, Burgos, Spain

Founded in the late 9th century, this architectural gem, which is still home to thirty Benedictine monks who dedicate their lives to work and prayer, is visited by thousands of people every year. It has been declared a World Heritage site.

98 Grand Mosque, Bobo Dioulasso, Burkina Faso

The city's mosque is built in what is known as the 'Sudanese style', which is very widespread in sub-Saharan Africa. Economical and simple, the walls and minarets are built of readily available materials including clay, earth, straw and gravel, strengthened with stakes and thick reeds.

99 Great Mosque, Kairouan, Tunisia

The fourth most important Islamic holy city after Mecca, Fez and Jerusalem, Kairouan was founded by Arabs in the 7th century. Seven pilgrimages to the city are equivalent to one Hajj, the pilgrimage to Mecca.

100–101 Shwedagon Pagoda, Yangon, Myanmar

Though legend has it that it is over 2,500 years old, it is thought that Shwedagon Pagoda, the holiest Buddhist stupa in Myanmar, was in fact built between the 6th and 10th centuries by two merchants who had received eight of the Buddha's hairs.

102 San Andrés Xecul, Guatemala

Nobody knows when or by whom this colourful church in the 'popular baroque' style was built, but with its façade painted in all the colours of the local güipil and decorated with saints, angels, cherubs and the two tigers at the top, it has become the pride of the Mayan people.

103 Ruwanweliseya Dagoba, Anuradhapura, Sri Lanka

In spite of the simplicity of its construction, the Ruwanweliseya Dagoba is considered to be one of the most beautiful stupas in the country, and Buddhist services continue to be held there.

104 Borobudur, Magelang, Java, Indonesia

The temples of Borobudur date back to the 9th century, and are popular pilgrimage sites. During the full moon in May, the three most important events in the life of the Buddha are celebrated: his birth, his enlightenment and his death which, according to the sacred texts, all took place on the same date.

105 Ladakh, India

On the roads in the Himalayas it is common to come across Buddhist chortens, small constructions which contain the remains of a lama saint, relics or a statue of Buddha. Travellers should always pass them on the left-hand side.

106–107 Tengboche Monastery, Nepal

In the region of Solo Khumbu, on the way to Everest, stands this Buddhist monastery, surrounded by spectacular landscape. The monks live in total isolation, dedicating their lives to study and meditation.

OFFERINGS, IMAGES, SYMBOLS

Ever since ancient times, invisible holiness has been expressed in visible images. Religious people have frequently articulated the impalpable elements of their faith in tangible offerings. Images of the divine and active demonstrations of faith belong to a symbolic world that ranges from the animal sacrifices and votive gifts of produce of earlier times to the interiorization of the image in the form of icons, and the spiritualization of the offering in the form of candles, incense and allegorical objects.

This entire symbolic world, apart from being an expression of faith, can also be pure superstition – the opposite of gods are idols, and behind myths and rites lie ideologies. Again we run into the familiar ambiguity: in the name of a god people indulge in ascetic privation; in the name of a god innocents are sacrificed. Throughout the history of religion, religiosity has often been marred by seeing offerings and sacrifices as the commercial and legal interpretation of our relationship with divinity. The first can be expressed as quid pro quo – I give to you in order that you give to me. As a Brahmin ritual has it: 'Here is the butter. What do you give me in exchange?' The second makes the mistake of attempting to placate supposed divine wrath by sacrificing victims. A mature, developed spirituality enables cultures to overcome both of these ideas.

The world of the sacred is incomprehensible if we do not pay close attention to symbolism, because symbols, myths and rites all involve (as Paul Ricoeur's philosophy reveals) polysemy and paradox. A symbol neither explains, nor silences; instead, it sets in motion a proccess of revealing beginning with a suggestion. This idea is echoed

Myanmar *A Buddhist offering, Mandalay*

in the description Heraclitus gives of the enigmatic oracle at Delphi: 'She does not tell you anything, neither does she conceal it, but rather she insinuates'. She helps to reveal sacredness, but she also hides it. To interpret her words, one needs to go beyond simply deciphering their meaning; what is necessary (as Ricoeur reminds us in his 1965 *De l'interpretation, Du Seuil*) is a method that works through suspecting. Given the ambiguity of symbolic manifestations in the name of something sacred, 'we find ourselves today in the situation of people who have not yet allowed their idols to die, while we are only just beginning to decipher the symbols'.

Images, offerings and symbols in the name of a god: are they vehicles of faith or a crossroads of different interests? Certainly Jesus criticized the rich who ostentatiously showed off the donations they gave in the temple – and praised the poor widow who donated her heartfelt, modest offering without anyone noticing her.

By the noon-day brightness,
And by the night when it darkeneth!
Thy Lord hath not forsaken thee,
Neither hath he been displeased.

And surely the Future
Shall be better for thee than the Past,
And in the end shall thy Lord be bounteous
To thee and thou be satisfied.

Did he not find thee an orphan and gave thee a home?
And found thee erring and guided thee,
And found thee needy and enriched thee.

As to the orphan therefore wrong him not;
And as to him that asketh of thee, chide him not away;
And as for the favours of thy Lord tell them abroad.

THE QUR'AN, 93

Above *Bangkok, Thailand*

Above *Pura Besakih, Bali, Indonesia*

Above *Tibet*

Above *Ise Shrine, Mie Prefecture, Japan*

137

Above *Our Lady of Guadalupe, Mexico City, Mexico*

Above *Akodessewa Market, Lomé, Togo* • 140–41 *Pushkar, India* • 142–3 *Katmandu, Nepal* • 144–5 *Erdene Zu Monastery, Mongolia*

139

Above *Meoto Iwa, Japan* • Opposite *Jokhang Temple, Lhasa, Tibet* • 148–9 *Lago Manasarovar, Tibet* • 150–51 *Mount Kailash, Tibet*

146

Above *Yardenit, Israel* • Opposite *Oueme river, Benin* • 158 *Synagogue, Barcelona, Spain* • 159 *Barcelona, Spain* • 160–61 *Varanasi, India*

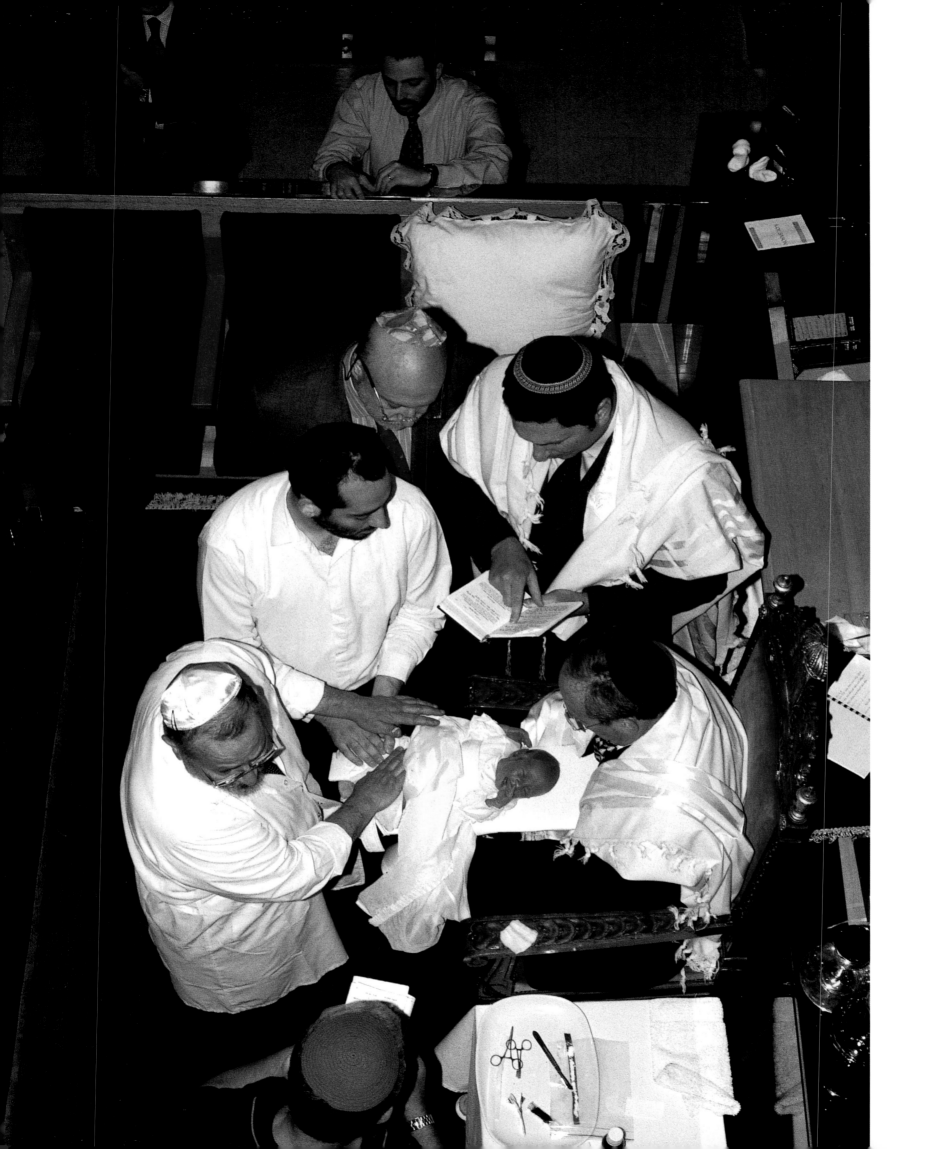

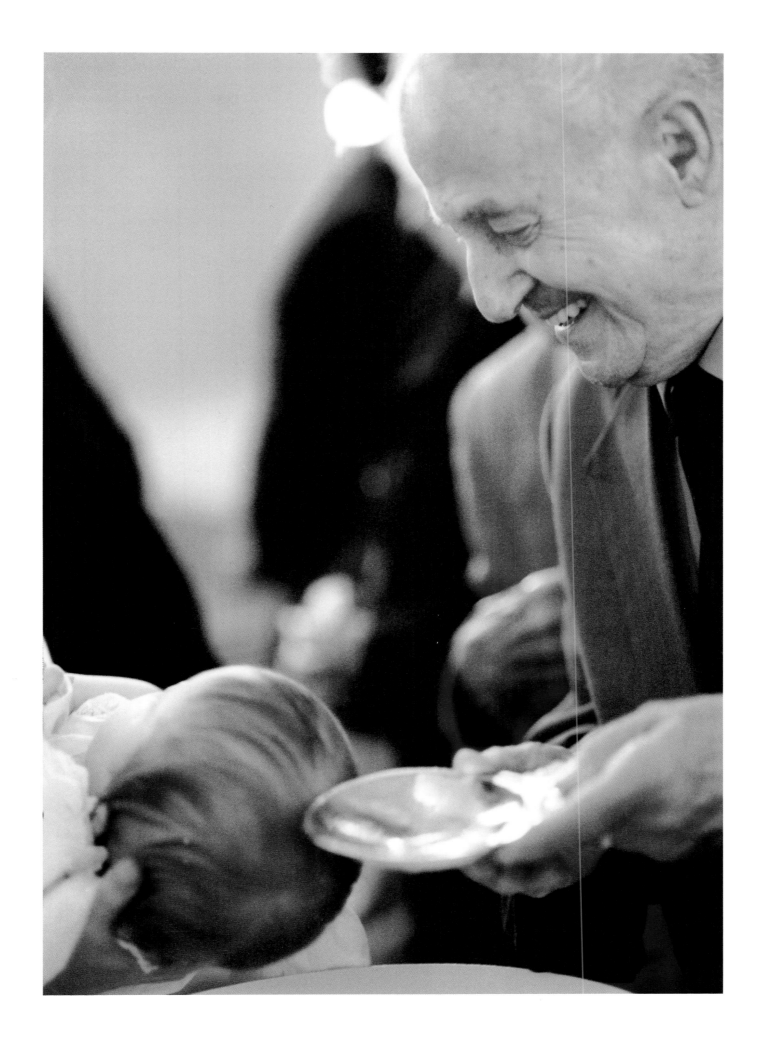

115 San Miguel Chicaj, Guatemala

Religion has played a very important part in the history of humanity. While for some it has been the driving force of human growth, for others it continues to be an obstacle to development. Thirty-three per cent of humanity is Christian, 22 per cent Muslim, 15 per cent Hindu, 6 per cent Buddhist, 4 per cent follow the Chinese traditional religion, 3 per cent is animist, 3 per cent follow other, smaller religions and 14 per cent do not believe in any kind of god.

116–17 Uluwatu Temple, Bali, Indonesia

The Kekak Hindu ceremony, which takes place at sunset.

118–19 Potala Palace, Lhasa, Tibet

Potala Palace is the archetypal symbol of Tibetan Buddhism. Built on an enormous hill in the centre of the city, it played a key important role in the administration of Tibet.

120 Pagan, Myanmar

Despite the fact that the written documents on the Buddha's life are filled with myths, legends and symbolism, that he existed is historical fact. The Buddha was the Indian prince Siddharta Gautama, who came from the caste of warriors and noblemen.

121 Luang Prabang, Laos

A Buddhist monk presents an offering. Many people in the West view Buddhism merely as a philosophy, a way of life or a technique for personal development rather than as a religion.

122 Varanasi, India

In the Aarti ceremony, held on the banks of the Ganges at nightfall, Hindus worship the river with oil lamps. Originally a very simple ceremony, it has now become a popular spectacle for tourists.

123 Santo Domingo, Guatemala City, Guatemala

The early 19th-century neoclassical church and monastery of Santo Domingo contains the image of Christ reclining, which is visited throughout the year by devotees bringing offerings. In some religions, offerings containing fire are a symbol of transformation, purification and regeneration.

124 Kiev, Ukraine

Basile Klimachtchouk takes care of the chapel of the Orthodox monastery of Sviato-Feodosievski. Following the collapse of the Soviet Union, religion has gained new importance in Eastern European countries.

125 Mount Emei, Sichuan Province, China

Buddhism was introduced into the area around Mount Emei in the 1st century AD. According to legend, Buddha Samantabhadra practised his rites in this area. There are now about 30 temples in the area around the mountain.

126 Chak Chak, Yazd, Iran

Chak Chak, also known as Pir-e Sabz, is located 50 kilometres (30 miles) from Yazd, and is one of the most important sanctuaries in Zoroastrianism. Every June, members of the faithful come from all over Iran to celebrate the Zoroastrian New Year before a flame that has been burning for centuries.

127 Tibet

Mahayana Buddhism arrived in Tibet in the 8th century. Until then, the region had been dominated by an animist religion, which was transformed and ended up exerting great influence over Buddhism.

128 Bali, Indonesia

A Hindu fire ceremony. Fire has played an integral part in the holy rites of almost every ancient culture. Sacred fire acts as a link between man's consciousness and cosmic consciousness.

129 Saigon Cathedral, Vietnam

Owing to the influence of the different peoples who have passed through this region, Vietnam has a considerable mixture of religions. Buddhism, Taoism, Confucianism, Catholicism and animism coexist without any problems.

130–131 Chichicastenango, Guatemala

On the hill of Pascual Abaj, the Mayan shamans carry out rituals and make offerings to the gods on behalf of people who come seeking to be cured of illness, good luck in business or happiness in love.

132 Sulawesi, Indonesia

In the Toradja people's animist burial rituals, the number of buffalos or pigs sacrificed depends on the social class of the deceased; the government has imposed taxes on each animal to prevent the decimation of herds.

133 Basilica of Our Lady of Pilar, Zaragoza, Spain

Altar boys present children to the image of the Virgin in the basilica of Our Lady of Pilar – the largest baroque church in Spain – and which some consider to be the first church devoted to the Marian cult in Christianity.

134 Bangkok, Thailand

The worship of spirits (phis), which predates Buddhism, is still common among the Thai people, who make offerings of all kinds such as releasing caged birds to ensure the protection of the spirits and a harmonious life.

135 Pura Besakih, Bali, Indonesia

Located on the slopes of Mount Agung, Pura Besakih is one of the largest temples in Indonesia. Here, flowers are offered to the the gods.

136 Tibet

Four main lineages or schools exist in Tibetan Buddhism. Lineage is very important, as it guarantees that the teachings stay alive; that is, that they have been transmitted from master to disciple ever since the times of the Buddha, always taught in a pure, readily understandable way.

137 Ise Shrine, Mie Prefecture, Japan

At the entrance to the Ise Shrine, the Miko san gives visitors an Omamori (talisman) – almost every Japanese carries one with them – or an Ema, a piece of votive wood to say 'thank you' for the favour granted. The concept of 'selling' is not sufficient for the Japanese; these objects are given as an 'exchange for cash donations' given by the visitor, and which is effectively equal to the price of what they take away with them.

138 Our Lady of Guadalupe, Mexico City, Mexico

The sanctuary of Our Lady of Guadalupe is one of the most sacred places for Mexicans. The building is home to the image of the Virgin that was engraved on a sheet of maguey cloth when she appeared before the Indian Juan Diego in December 1531, ten years after the conquest of Mexico. Pope Pius XII called the Virgin the 'Empress of the Americas', and John Paul II beatified Juan Diego.

139 Akodessewa Market, Lomé, Togo

In Akodessewa fetish market, one can find all kinds of potions, amulets and dead animals used in the practice of magic and voodoo.

140–41 Pushkar, India

These sacred trees can be found in temples throughout India, and they are thought to grant wishes. Wishes are made by tying a piece of thread or cloth onto the branches. Those who want children, for example, hang a little cot on a branch.

142–3 Kathmandu, Nepal

A Brahmin or Hindu priest – with his head shaved as a sign of humility – helps a devotee, with all his paraphernalia, to carry out the sacred rites on the banks of the River Bhagmati, in front of the Pashupatinath Temple.

144–5 Erdene Zu Monastery, Mongolia

Due to the lack of flowers in the area, khatas (long silk scarves or handkerchiefs, either white or in different colours) are given as offerings or as a sign of welcome and respect.

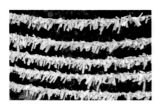

146 Meoto Iwa, Japan

Omikuji – little pieces of paper hung on branches – can be bought in Shinto temples. They tell your fortune, but if the prediction is not good, you can leave it hanging on a branch. Shintoism was the state religion before the Second World War, closely associated with the Emperor. After the war, many Shintoist religious practices were abandoned.

147 Jokhang Temple, Lhasa, Tibet

The Buddhist temple of Jokhang is the final destination in Lhasa of Tibetan pilgrims. According to legend, it was built on an ancient lake, after which every temple built in the area collapsed.

148–9 Lake Manasarovar, Tibet

All pilgrims who bathe in the sacred waters of this lake are cleansed of all their sins. Meanwhile, if you walk all the way around the lake and you find a feather, a pebble or small fish, you will have a life of plenty.

150–51 Mount Kailash, Tibet

The holiest mountain in Asia, Mount Kailash in Tibet is the home of the god Shiva and his consort. It is worshipped by Hindus, Buddhists, Jainists and Sikhs. The complete pilgrimage lasts for six weeks, in very harsh weather conditions, though some pilgrims take several years to complete it.

152 San Juan, Puerto Rico

This bronze statue in the Plazuela de la Rogativa, in Old San Juan, commemorates the torchlit religious procession that the English invaders mistook for reinforcements, causing them to flee.

153 Grand Popo, Benin

This village, which stands on the same coast from which African slaves were sent to America, is considered to be one of the birthplaces of voodoo. Visitors can attend authentic ceremonies and see animals sacrificed and 'straw ghosts' dance.

154–5 Konya, Turkey

The semas or dervish dances are performed by the members of a mystical Sufi order in Konya. By spinning quickly like a top they attempt to escape from earthly life to reach a mystical union with the great beyond.

156 Yardenit, Israel

All year round, this kibbutz in Yardenit organizes baptisms for Christian believers in the waters of the River Jordan. The ceremony involves complete immersion, and many of those who undergo find it an extremely moving experience .

157 Oueme river, Benin

As a result of the large number of Evangelical churches in Africa, baptism by immersion in rivers has become common. These ceremonies are extremely popular with the faithful.

158 Synagogue, Barcelona, Spain

Circumcision is a ritual carried out on Jewish boys when they are eight days old, in a ceremony attended only by men. This precept has been compulsory ever since Abraham was circumcised, following a divine order, almost 6,000 years ago.

159 Barcelona, Spain

The Catholic ritual of baptism – washing away Original Sin and giving the child faith and divine life – has evolved over time. Here newborn María Rubio is baptized by her grandfather Enrique.

160–61 Varanasi, India

Located on the right bank of the River Ganges (the left bank is considered impure and nothing is built there) is the city of Varanasi, dedicated to the god Shiva. Every year it is visited by millions of Hindu pilgrims who come to bathe in the water and even to die. The bathing ritual offers liberation from the cycle of reincarnation.

168–9 *Stonehenge, Wiltshire, England* • Above *Trepucó, Menorca, Spain*

Above *Tikal, Guatemala* • 172–3 *Machu Picchu, Peru* • 174–5 *Uluru (Ayers Rock), Australia* • 176–7 *Mount Everest, Nepal*
178–9 *Amboseli National Park, Kenya* • 180 *Yosemite National Park, California, United States* • 181 *Sulawesi, Indonesia* • 182–3 *Montserrat, Spain*
184 *Great Meteoron Monastery, Kalampaka, Greece* • 185 *Mount Popa, Myanmar* • 186–7 *Easter Island, Chile*

188 *Meoto-Iwa, Futami, Japan* • 189 *Itsukushima Shrine, Itsukushima, Japan*

Above *Tiwanaku, Bolivia*

Above *Pyramid of the Sun, Teotihuacan, Mexico* • 202–203 *Pagan, Myanmar*

168–9 Stonehenge, Wiltshire, England

It is not known who built this megalithic construction between 3000 and 1000 BC, nor what its purpose was, though many think that it was a temple to the sun god or a sacrifice site.

178–9 Amboseli National Park, Kenya

The volcanic Kilimanjaro, at 5,895 metres (19,340 feet), is the tallest mountain in Africa and a sacred site for the tribes of the region. The Masai call it Ngaje Ngai, or 'House of God'. Others do not give it a name, but only refer the white side (Kibo), a sign of eternity and good luck, and the black side (Mawenzi), associated with the forces of evil.

170 Trepucó, Menorca, Spain

In the Talayotic town of Trepucó, which dates back to 1300 BC, this structure called a taula was used as both altar and funerary monument. Archeologists have linked the orientation of the stones with the constellations in the sky.

180 Yosemite National Park, California, United States

Now a National Park, Yosemite (the place of 'the open tongue' according to native languages) was a sacred valley for the Ahwahneechee Native American Indians.

171 Tikal, Guatemala

This complex of Mayan pyramids and religious buildings, which was only discovered in 1848, was built in around 200 BC; three centuries later it had grown to be a town with some 100,000 inhabitants. However, in the 9th century it began to fall into decline, together with the rest of the lowland Mayan civilizations, for reasons that have never fully been understood.

181 Sulawesi, Indonesia

In the Tana Toraja region they believe that the dead can take their belongings to the next life. Huge tombs are excavated out of the rock walls with balconies containing 'Tau tau', wooden statues representing the dead.

172–3 Machu Picchu, Peru

Discovered in 1911, the amazing city of the Incas was built in around 1450 as a military fortress, although the fact that the human remains that have been found have been mostly of women has led some to think that it was a refuge of the 'virgins of the sun'.

182–3 Montserrat, Spain

The Benedictine monastery on the mountain of Montserrat is home to the image of the Virgin known as 'La Moreneta', the patron saint of Catalonia. The mountain – considered a holy site given that the Virgin appeared there in AD 880 – also has several caves and hermitages.

174–5 Uluru (Ayers Rock), Australia

Situated in Uluru-Kata Tjuta National Park, this massive rock, measuring 3.6 kilometres (2 miles) long by 348 metres (1,140 feet) high, possesses enormous spiritual significance for the Anangu. In recent years this has led to tension with visitors who have used it for mountaineering, since the Anangu believe that it would be a bad omen if someone were to be injured or die there.

184 Great Meteoron Monastery, Kalampaka, Greece

The wide flatlands of Thessaly form the backdrop to these amazing granite columns on which the Byzantine monasteries of Meteora were built in the 14th century. Twenty-two monasteries were constructed, which were inhabited by stylos (literally, 'column') communities. The Great Meteoron Monastery is the most outstanding of them all.

176–7 Mount Everest, Nepal

Known to the Chinese and Tibetans as Chomolungma ('Mother of the World'), the tallest mountain on earth is considered sacred by many people in the region. All mountain ascents here begin with a ceremony for the mountain gods.

185 Mount Popa, Myanmar

At a height of 1,519 metres (4,985 feet), the sanctuary of Mount Popa is the home of the 37 main nats (spirits). Twice a year, coinciding with the full moons in May and November, thousands of believers climb the mountain via a steep stairway dotted with small temples and altars, and leave offerings.

186–7 Easter Island, Chile

Mystery still surrounds the Moai statues of this isolated island in the Pacific, where a civilization died out completely, though it seems that they were built to worship ancestors.

188 Meoto-Iwa, Futami, Japan

The Meoto-Iwa (the 'Married Rocks') are two holy rocks near the sanctuary of Okitama that jut out of the sea; they represent the husband and wife, and are joined by a rope called the shimenawa.

189 Itsukushima Shrine, Itsukushima, Japan

The Itsukushima Shrine dates back to AD 593. The beauty of the spot and the work of the monks to maintain the temples has made it one of the most beautiful of Shintoist sites.

190 Moon Island, Lake Titicaca, Bolivia

During the age of the Inca Empire, Moon Island (also known as Coati Island) was the site of a temple or 'Palace of the Virgins'. It was inhabited by women, who might become second wives or human sacrifices. The only man allowed onto the island was the Emperor.

191 Erdene Zu Monastery, Kharkhorin, Mongolia

Erdene Zu was the first Buddhist monastery in Mongolia. Construction began in 1586 and it was completed three centuries later. At its zenith, this important Buddhist centre contained almost one hundred temples and was home to more than one thousand monks.

192–3 St Catherine's Monastery, Mount Sinai, Egypt

This Orthodox monastery, built at a height of 1,570 metres (5,150 feet), was founded after the persecution of the anchorites in the 4th century. It is built on the site where, legend has it, Moses saw the burning bush.

194–5 Ladakh, India

This ancient kingdom is known as the 'Land of the Moon'. Responding to the strong Buddhist tradition, monasteries flourished throughout the area.

196–7 Bamiyan, Afghanistan

A radical interpretation of Islam's prohibition of images depicting the human form led Afghanistan's Taliban government, in 2001, to destroy the two Buddhist figures carved out of the rock. One of them was the largest in the world, some 53 metres (174 feet) high.

198–9 Temple of the Sun, Colorado, United States

The Temple of the Sun, which stands in the ruins of Mesa Verde, Colorado, was built in the deep canyons by the Anasazi Indians out of mud and stones some 400 years ago. It was here that they held their animist ceremonies.

200 Tiwanaku, Bolivia

The 'Statue of the Friar' in the temple of Kalasaya, seen among the ruins of the city of Tiwanaku, the capital of the mighty pre-Inca civilization. The Incas believed it was the place where man was created, and from where the god Viracocha reigned.

201 Pyramid of the Sun, Teotihuacan, Mexico

The Pyramid of the Sun, the third tallest structure of its kind in the world, was built in around AD 100, using three million tons of rocks and brick. It is thought that its four sides used to be covered with brightly painted stucco.

202–203 Pagan, Myanmar

The 'City of a Million Temples' dates back to the 10th century. For the next two hundred years, one king after another vied to build more temples than his predecessor until, in 1287, Kublai Khan and his hordes invaded the country, and most of the temples were demolished. The Second World War put paid to the rest. Fortunately, in recent times, local religious fervour has led to the beginning of the reconstruction of this amazing city.

THE PARADOX OF INTERPRETATION

Hands raised and faces turned toward the sky in a supplicating manner at a lively meeting suggest a beyond that seems to be up there somewhere, above the clouds. Meanwhile, heads and torsos bent down in prayer in the mosque are facing a beyond that seems to be located in the centre of the earth. This paradoxical contrast suggests sacredness at the same time as blurring it.

There is an equally paradoxical contrast between the red blood on a bullfighter's suit and the sober, calmness of the cloak in the image of mercy. A matador prays in the chapel before the start of a bullfight, in which the artistic is mixed with the painful. Is this an example of devout religiousness or superstitious magic? Perhaps anthropological studies can explain it better than theology can.

But the greatest paradox lies in the photos where prayer overlaps with war. In one photograph we can see a soldier praying before the Western Wall in Jerusalem, hands clasped together and head bowed. In the name of which god is someone acting when he is capable of intoning a psalm of peace before taking up arms?

A young soldier kneels down before a uniformed priest, who is identified by the purple stole that he wears over his camouflage outfit. Is the young man fighting because he has been inculcated with the idea that he is helping to 'free the people'? How does a soldier reconcile his profession with his religion? What prayer does someone pray when preparing to fight? Perhaps a prayer for good judgment with respect to the Sixth Commandment, or perhaps one for the enemies he must confront the next day. And the priest who blesses him? What is the nature of his blessing on those who kill and may be killed? In the name of which god does someone kneel when he is about to open fire?

With these photographs, we return to the theme that has served as the main thread since the introduction: in the name of a god, people both care for the dying and kill innocents; in the name of a god, peace is made and violence unleashed. From Cain and Abel to

India *Meditating by the Ganges at Varanasi*

Afghanistan and Iraq, humanity has always been enmeshed in fratricidal conflict. Human beings, who believe themselves to be rational, are animals that are both vulnerable and capable of causing physical harm; able to destroy themselves and to annihilate others.

We need a catharsis following the impact of all these paradoxes of sacredness, and it comes in the form of the photograph of Tibetan children, calmly studying the words of the sutras that enter through their eyes and their ears, pacifying them and turning them into pacifiers.

The submitting men, the submitting women,
The believing men, the believing women,
The obedient men, the obedient women,
The truthful men, the truthful women,
The steadfast men, the steadfast women,
The reverent men, the reverent women,
The charitable men, the charitable women,
The fasting men, the fasting women,
The chaste men, the chaste women,
And the men who commemorate God frequently,
    and the commemorating women;
God has prepared for them forgiveness
    and a great recompense.

THE QUR'AN, 33: 35

The Tao that can be told is not the eternal Tao.
The name that can be named is not the eternal
Name. The unnameable is the eternally real.

TAO TE CHING, I, 45

208 *Lalibela, Ethiopia* • 209 *Solo Khumbu, Nepal* • 210 *Mandalay, Myanmar* • 211 *Timbuktu, Mali* • 212–13 *Anuradhapura, Sri Lanka*
Above *Swayambhu Stupa, Kathmandu, Nepal* • Opposite *Jama Masjid, New Delhi, India*

214

Above *Shiraz, Iran*

DONATED BY
SHLOMO, FAYGE, MICHAL, ARIELLA,
RACHELLI, AZRIEL & MOSHE
ZAKHEIM
BROOKLYN, N.Y.

Above *Livingstone, Zambia*

208 Lalibela, Ethiopia

The origins of Christianity in Ethiopia are still under discussion. Some believe that the religion derived from Africans who had been in Jerusalem and met Jesus there; others believe that St Matthew passed through the country, bringing the faith with him. And others say that it was two shipwrecked Palestinians who spread the faith, on the orders of the king.

209 Solo Khumbu, Nepal

Originally, communities of Buddhist monks dedicated their lives to the search for personal salvation, supported by the local people to whom they taught the Dharma, or the teachings of the Buddha. Nowadays, these monks are more involved in alleviating poverty, taking care of the sick and education.

210 Mandalay, Myanmar

The Mon people, who where the first inhabitants of Burma (today Myanmar), originally practised Theravada Buddhism, which they learned from the missions sent by the Indian Emperor Asoka in around 300 BC. Today, 87 per cent of the country's population is Buddhist.

211 Timbuktu, Mali

Children studying the Qur'an from wooden books, at the entrance of a Qur'anic school or Madrassa.

212–13 Anuradhapura, Sri Lanka

In the middle of the largest of the ancient cities of Sri Lanka stands Mirisavatiya Dagoba, built around 2,000 years ago and a faithful reflection of the island's conversion to Buddhism.

214 Swayambhu Stupa, Kathmandu, Nepal

Built on a small hill around 2,500 years ago, Swayambhu stupa has etched on its four harmikas (sides) the eyes of the Buddha, signifying that he sees everything. Beneath the eyes can be seen the Nepalese symbol ek, which means 'unity'.

215 Jama Masjid, New Delhi, India

A female devotee reading the Qur'an in the Jama Masjid. In mosques, women are segregated from men; they are not allowed to read or pray in the main hall, and after nightfall they cannot enter the building.

216 Shiraz, Iran

These mullahs (scholars of the Qur'an, the Hadith and Islamic law) are members of the Shi'ite clergy, which is headed by the ayatollahs; they wear black cloaks and turbans if they are descendants of the Prophet Muhammad, and white garments if not.

217 Jerusalem, Israel

The ceremony of the Bar Mitzvah ('Son of the Commandment') is held for all Jewish boys when they reach the age of 13, after they have studied religion and the fundamentals of the Jewish life for a year. They wear the tefillin and the tallit for the first time, and are allowed to read publicly from the Torah.

218–19 Guatemala City, Guatemala

The crisis of traditional Christianity, especially in rich countries, has led to a flourishing of 'charismatic' churches, often dominated by a single personality.

220–21 Tehran, Iran

Prayers on Friday – the most important day of the week for Muslims – at the mosque at Teheran University.

226–7 Lima, Peru

The Christian cross was brought to South America by the Spanish conquistadores, and even though the clergy who came with them fought against Inca polytheism, the result has been a type of religious syncretism.

222 Jerusalem, Israel

The Western Wall is the most famous site in Judaism. It is part of the temple that was built by Herod the Great, and devotees come here to pray, men and women separately. Small paper notes with prayers written on them are stuffed into cracks in the wall. As a consequence, the former national telephone company Bezeq has provided a fax number available throughout the world; once a day, some 100 messages are collected and taken to the wall, free of charge, by an employee.

228 Livingstone, Zambia

The Evangelical churches are gaining more followers in Africa every day. Here a pastor studies the Bible with his flock on a Sunday.

229 Isfahan, Iran

Anonymous prayer in the Sheik Lotfallah mosque. Muslims must pray five times a day in a clean place, facing Mecca.

223 Mostar, Bosnia and Herzegovina

A chaplain in the Spanish army receives confession from a soldier before he enters into service.

230 Ladakh, India

Inside the prayer wheel there are mantras and sacred texts engraved which, owing to their divine origin, are effective ways of communicating with the gods. The devotee turns the wheel clockwise, using the right hand to liberate the powers of the sacred texts.

224 Seville, Spain

According to bullfighting tradition, before the fight, the matador asks the saints for protection in his duel.

231 Varanasi, India

A sadhu, a disciple of Shiva in one of the city's ghats. The sick and elderly make pilgrimages to the city because, according to Hinduism, anyone who dies here or within a certain distance of the spot will be freed from the cycle of reincarnation, and will enter nirvana directly.

225 Kiev, Ukraine

The Orthodox Church in Kiev managed to survive both the destruction of the city by the Mongols, in the year 1240, and the years of Soviet domination. Today the faith has come back to life, although owing to internal problems it is now divided into three Patriarchates.

232–3 Pagan, Myanmar

At daybreak every morning, the monks wander the streets carrying small bowls in which the faithful place their offerings in the form of food for the monks to eat.

There is a mystery, beneath abstraction, silent,
depthless, alone, unchanging, ubiquitous and
liquid, the mother of nature. It has no name,
but I call it 'the Way'.

TAO TE CHING, 25, 69

The Tao is like a well: used but never used up.
It is like the eternal void: filled with infinite
possibilities. It is hidden but always present.
I don't know who gave birth to it.
It is older than God.

TAO TE CHING, 4, 45

EPILOGUE

On finishing my journey through the pages of this book, I have the sensation of having visited a museum that is stuffed full of valuable pieces. The result is, I feel, quite densely packed – the second time you, the reader, choose to wander through the book's five halls, you should take a closer, more relaxed look at some of the images and, keeping the introductory comments in mind, savour the fascinating and powerful duality of sacredness. Just like a kaleidoscope, the variety and multiplicity is enormous, but with just one slight movement, the whole picture changes: the praying face becomes a threatening one, and the fervent procession explodes into an uncontrollable riot.

When the publisher of this book first suggested that I write this commentary, I felt unsure and a little puzzled. The history of religion is such a broad, even multicoloured, subject that the idea of trying to explore it all was a little frightening. You cannot have many close friends, and something similar happens with religions. Yet if I only know my own religion, then my spirituality is impoverished. Making the effort to understand, from within, one or two other religions both helps me and widens the horizon of religiosity itself. But life is short, and I do not have enough time to make the same effort truly to understand all religions, and hence my hesitation as to whether I could really contribute to this project. But the highly intuitive Andrés Gamboa, instead of wasting time trying to persuade me, simply placed a few contrasting photographs on the table: the soldier praying with his machine gun, the priest and the penitent, both in uniform, celebrating a sacrament of reconciliation before entering into battle; the Buddha in meditation; the Virgin of Fátima…. What could be done with these photos? They are neither an apology for peace, nor propaganda for war; instead, they force us to think about the ambiguity of religions, and urge us to decide, and to choose one way or the other.

My perplexity turned into enthusiasm for the possibility of doing something with this kaleidoscope of sacredness. At that time I had not met the journalist and photographer Eduardo Rubio, but instead knew him only by name and from his photos that I had seen in other publications. And now, as I wander once more through this five-hall museum, my initial feeling is confirmed: I am not an expert in photography, nor do I pretend to be an art critic, but for me, Eduardo's style has an extraordinary capacity for surprising the polyhedral sense of reality, and especially for capturing in a snapshot those moments of double meaning that raise questions in our minds. His photos give us food for thought, and the ability to think critically and creatively about spirituality is precisely one of the faculties we need to develop in this world that is increasingly plagued by fundamentalism.

JUAN MASIÁ CLAVEL

ACKNOWLEDGMENTS

Soon after returning from a long, difficult journey on the Trans-Siberian Railway, through Russia, Mongolia and China, and promptly beginning work on the completion of this volume, I suffered a heart attack that almost sent me off into the 'next world' that I had been exploring for three years. The efforts of Yvonne Turull, who proved to be much more than a friend, and the casualty department and intensive care unit at the Clínica Teknon in Barcelona, made it possible for me to carry on in this world, and to complete this book. I would like to thank them all, and especially the doctors Jorge Ríus, Gerardo Maqueda and Belén Gualis.

This volume is the result of the work of many people who collaborated on it, either directly or indirectly. Thus, in fact, it has many authors, the names of whom I would have been delighted to have seen on the front cover alongside mine.

From the beginning the project was backed by the support, faith and hopes of Juan Carlos Luna, Managing Director of Lunwerg Editores, Andrés Gamboa, Editor-in-Chief, and Bettina Benet, the project's designer. I would like to express my thanks to all three, and my admiration for their work.

Travelling through so many countries involved an enormous amount of complicated planning – aeroplane tickets, visas, hotels – which could only be achieved by the finest professionals: Nóbel Tours and Indoriente. Thus I would like to thank Roberto and Antonio Peregrin, the managers of the companies and the people behind all my movements. As well as their friendship, they have also made available to me their exceptional teams of staff.

As for the documentation process, one person who played a very important role was the young, brilliant journalist, Beatriz Fiestas Clapés, with whom I hope to continue working in the future.

My thanks, too, to Agustín Pániker (Editorial Kairós) for his advice on the subject.

I must thank a long list of journalists and friends to whom I will be eternally in debt for their helpful information and contacts: Rafael Poch (La Vanguardia, Beijing) and his wife Lourdes García (Catalunya Radio), Jaume Batroli (TV3), Pepe Verdú (Altaïr), Xavier Más de Xaxás (La Vanguardia), Rafa Manzano (Ser), María José Ramudo (RTVE), Pilar Blanco (Punto Radio), Félix Dot (Alessport) and Albert Solé Bruset.

The more than 50,000 photographs that I took were all shot on film using Nikon cameras and lenses. I would like to thank Finicon España and the members of its technical service, who were always ready to help me solve any problem.

I must not forget Casanova Profesional, whose staff were always ready to provide me with the latest items on the market; in the same way, I would like to thank the professional laboratories EGM in Barcelona, where all the images were processed, and my good friend Jaume Fernández, from MasMac – my computer guru.

To take these photos, I spent almost 700 hours in aeroplanes flying around the world. As a consequence, I would like to thank the following people working in different airlines for the help they gave me: Almudena López Amor from Air France and KLM; Cristina Pastor from Delta Airlines; Enrique Cernadas from Swissair; Antonio Huete from Varig; Ignacio Pascual from Aerolíneas Argentinas; Joaquín Martín from Thai; and Víctor Moneo, Carlos Martín and Laura Blanco from Iberia.

I am also indebted for the excellent service I received at the IURIS travel agency in Barcelona, and particularly from Carla Ferreri, Montse Gurri and Marina Serrano.

And to my old friend Germán Saret, from Saret&Ferrer, for his superb organization of my journey on the Tran-Siberian Railway.

Nina Fernández, from Hilton España, offered me all her support.

Dozens of friends, in different parts of the world, solved many problems for me during those three years of travelling.

The lovely doctor of Political Science, Ana Sofía Cardenal, in Guatemala.

Francisca Mérida in Madrid, and the Maza family and Carlos Telmo in Seville.

Montse Marí, always my 'salvation' in Japan.

Sujan Singh Pannu, my 'elder brother' and my finest adviser in India, and Massud Naderi, my 'little brother' in Iran.

Gabriel González de Kobo and Africae Safari, who skilfully transported me to many parts of Africa.

In Argentina, to Alejandro Amestoy and Cecilia Ursino from Cynsa. And to the Zunini family, who proved to be my warmest refuge in Buenos Aires, as were Rodrigo Soto in Chile, Bakary Camara in Ethiopia and Zhou Mi in China.

In addition, I would like to express my thanks for their support to Médicos Sin Fronteras and to Nuria Sonego, from the Comunidad Israelita of Barcelona. Thanks also to the Tibetan monks Wuang Cheng and Lobsang at the Tibetan community of Dharamsala.

Finally, my greatest thanks go to all those friends who supported me during my most difficult moments and experiences. Without them, this book would never have been possible.

EDUARDO RUBIO

Photographs from other sources

p. 33 *Maha Kumbh Mela, India.* © *Sophie Elbaz/ Sygma/Corbis*
p. 35 *Mecca, Saudi Arabia.* © *Kazuyoshi Nomachi/Corbis*
pp. 36–7 *Almonte, Spain. Jürgen Richter*

INDEX